2ⁿᵈ EDITION

Ventures 2

WORKBOOK

Gretchen Bitterlin   Dennis Johnson   Donna Price   Sylvia Ramirez

K. Lynn Savage (Series Editor)

with Deborah Gordon

CAMBRIDGE
UNIVERSITY PRESS

CAMBRIDGE
UNIVERSITY PRESS

University Printing House, Cambridge CB2 8BS, United Kingdom

One Liberty Plaza, 20th Floor, New York, NY 10006, USA

477 Williamstown Road, Port Melbourne, VIC 3207, Australia

4843/24, 2nd Floor, Ansari Road, Daryaganj, Delhi – 110002, India

79 Anson Road, #06–04/06, Singapore 079906

Cambridge University Press is part of the University of Cambridge.

It furthers the University's mission by disseminating knowledge in the pursuit of education, learning and research at the highest international levels of excellence.

www.cambridge.org
Information on this title: www.cambridge.org/9781107635388

First published 2008
20 19 18 17 16 15 14 13 12 11

Printed by Vivar Printing, Malaysia

A catalogue record for this publication is available from the British Library

ISBN 978-1-107-68722-6 Student's Book with Audio CD
ISBN 978-1-107-63538-8 Workbook with Audio CD
ISBN 978-1-139-87102-0 Online Workbook
ISBN 978-1-107-66579-8 Teacher's Edition with Assessment Audio CD / CD-ROM
ISBN 978-1-107-66009-0 Class Audio CDs
ISBN 978-1-107-67928-3 Presentation Plus

Additional resources for this publication at www.cambridge.org/ventures

Art direction, book design, photo research, and layout services: Q2A / Bill Smith
Audio production: CityVox, LLC

Illustration credits

John Batten: 18, 23, 30, 73, 75, 90, 101, 125

Mona Daly: 6, 33, 42, 66, 109

Chuck Gonzales: 13, 31, 38, 79, 105, 114

Ben Hasler: 20, 24, 80

Pamela Hobbs: 8, 16, 37

Peter Hoey: 53 (t), 85, 116

Images courtesy Precision Dynamics-St. John: 47 (t)

Frank Montagna: 9

Vilma Ortiz-Dillon: 11, 20, 32, 49, 54, 55, 70, 79, 83, 102

Q2A Media Services: 2, 49 (#4), 53 (b), 65, 77, 89, 113

Photography credits

Cover front (tl) Andrew Zarivny/Shutterstock, (tr) Stuart Monk/Shutterstock, (r) Gary D Ercole/Photolibrary/Getty Images, (cr) Sam Kolich, (br) Nathan Maxfield/iStockphoto, (c) Monkey Business Images/Shutterstock, (bl) Alistair Forrester Shankie/iStockphoto, (cl) ML Harris/Iconica/Getty Images, (l) Mark Lewis/Digital Vision/Getty Images, back (tc) cloki/Shutterstock, (br) gualtiero boffi/Shutterstock, 4 (cl) ©Masterfile, (bl) ©PhotoTalk/iStockphoto, (tr) ©Masterfile, 7 (cl) ©Lisa S./Shutterstock, 19 (cr) ©Khafizov Ivan Harisovich/Shutterstock, 21 (tl) ©Sadik Gulec/Shutterstock, (tcl) ©Christian Delbert/Shutterstock, (cl) ©Blaz Kure/Shutterstock, (bl) ©sixninepixels/Shutterstock, 25 (cl) ©dotshock/Shutterstock, (tcl) ©CandyBox Images/Shutterstock, (tcr) ©Joshua Hodge Photography/iStockphoto, (tr) ©Joel Eichler/iStockphoto, (bl) ©dotshock/Shutterstock, (bcl) ©Pressmaster/Shutterstock, (bcr) ©iStockphoto/

Thinkstock, (br) ©clearstockconcepts/iStockphoto, 26 (cr) ©Jose Luis Pelaez Inc/Alamy, 27 (cr) ©Max Topchii/Shutterstock, 29 (tl) ©Purestock/Getty Images, 39 (tl) ©Goodluz/Shutterstock, (bl) ©B2M Productions/Getty Images, 43 (c) ©Jerzyworks/Masterfile, 45 (br) ©Blaj Gabriel/Shutterstock, 47 (c) ©Monkey Business/Fotolia, 63 (tr) ©Masterfile, (br) ©Roy Mehta/Getty Images, 67 (cl) ©AVAVA/Shutterstock, 69 (tl) ©Blend Images/Masterfile, 78 (tl) ©pryzmat/Shutterstock, (tr) ©Supertrooper/Shutterstock, (cl) ©Creatas/Thinkstock, (c) ©ppart/Shutterstock, (cr) ©Masterfile, (bl) ©Diane Macdonald/Alamy, (bc) ©Neamov/Shutterstock, (br) ©Alexey Dudoladov/iStockphoto, 83 (tl) ©grekoff/Shutterstock, (cl) ©Serg64/Shutterstock, (bl) ©iStockphoto/Thinkstock, (tc) ©dny3d/Shutterstock, (c) ©John Kasawa/Shutterstock, (bc) ©sagir/Shutterstock, (tr) ©pockygallery/Shutterstock, (cr) ©Pakhnyushcha/Shutterstock, (br) ©iStockphoto/Thinkstock, 84 (tr) ©Kathrin

Ziegler/Getty Images, 97 (tl) ©Tom Hahn/iStockphoto, (tcl) ©Amy Myers/Shutterstock, (bcl) ©James Woodson/Thinkstock, (bl) ©Thomas Barwick/Getty Images, (tr) ©Tom England/iStockphoto, (tcr) ©kristian sekulic/iStockphoto, (bcr) ©FedorKondratenko/Shutterstock, (br) ©Jupiterimages/Thinkstock, 99 (tl) ©iStockphoto/Thinkstock, (tc) ©Hakan Caglav/iStockphoto, (tr) ©Fancy/Media Bakery, (bl) ©sjlocke/iStockphoto, (bc) ©Ann Marie Kurtz/iStockphoto, (br) ©Buccina Studios/Thinkstock, 104 (tl) ©BanksPhotos/iStockphoto, (tc) ©iStockphoto/Thinkstock, (tr) ©Andrew Howe/iStockphoto, 106 (tr) ©kurhan/Shutterstock, 117 (tl) ©Oktay Ortakcioglu/iStockphoto, (tr) ©iStockphoto/Thinkstock, (cl) ©siamionau pavel/Shutterstock, (cr) ©Ildi Papp/Shutterstock, (bl) ©Rob Byron/Shutterstock, (br) ©Richard M Lee/Shutterstock, 121 (bl) ©empathysympathy/Shutterstock, (bc) ©svetlana67/Fotolia, (br) ©Morgan Lane Photography/Shutterstock

Contents

Welcome

1 Meet your classmates

A What are the people doing? Complete the sentences. Use the words in the box.

help   read   speak   use   write

1. Bao _is reading_ a book.
2. Claudia _____ a computer.
3. Sara _____ on the phone.
4. Ana and Amy _____ on the board.
5. Wei _____ Raul with his homework.

B Complete the answers.

1. **A** Is Claudia reading?

   B _No_, _she isn't_ .

2. **A** Is Wei helping Raul with his homework?

   B _____, _____ .

3. **A** Is Sara sleeping?

   B _____, _____ .

4. **A** Are Ana and Amy reading?

   B _____, _____ .

5. **A** Is Claudia using a computer?

   B _____, _____ .

6. **A** Is Bao reading a book?

   B _____, _____ .

Check your answers. See page 132.

2 Skills

A Read the sentences. Look at the chart. Circle T (True) or F (False). Then correct the false statements.

Skill	Ivan	Irma	Oscar	Lara	Joe	Sandy
speak Spanish		✓				
speak Chinese						✓
cook			✓			
iron					✓	
swim				✓		
use a computer	✓	✓				
drive a truck		✓				✓

1. Ivan can cook.   T   (F)   _Ivan can't cook._

2. Lara can't speak Spanish.   T   F   _____

3. Ivan and Irma can speak Chinese.   T   F   _____

4. Irma can't iron.   T   F   _____

5. Joe can swim.   T   F   _____

6. Sandy can drive a truck.   T   F   _____

7. Oscar and Lara can use a computer.   T   F   _____

8. Irma can't drive a truck.   T   F   _____

B Listen to the conversation. Check Lisa's skills.

TRACK 2

✓ speak English   ____ write Chinese

____ speak Chinese   ____ use computers

____ drive a truck   ____ cook

3 Verb tense review (present and past of *be* verb)

A Complete the story. Use *am*, *is*, *are*, *was*, *were*, and *weren't*.

My name ___is___ Rafael. I _____ from
        1.   2.
El Salvador. My wife's name _____ Celia. She
                                    3.
_____ from El Salvador, too. There _____
    4.   5.
two children in our family – one son and one

daughter. Our son, Tomás, _____ 13 years old.
                                  6.
Our daughter, Claudia, _____ 14 years old.
                            7.
Tomás and Claudia _____ born in the U.S. Celia and I _____ born in the U.S.
                        8.   9.
We _____ born in El Salvador.
      10.

    Tomás and Claudia _____ students. They _____ both very smart!
                            11.   12.
I _____ a teacher in El Savador, but now I _____ a cook. Celia _____ a
    13.   14.   15.
nurse in El Salvador, but now she _____ a student, just like Tomás and Claudia.
                                      16.
We _____ all very busy, but we _____ very happy.
      17.   18.

B Read the chart. Complete the sentences.

	What is your name?	Where are you from?	What was your occupation there?	Are you married?	How many people are in your family?
1.	Diego	Mexico	truck driver	Yes	five
2.	Bae	Korea	student	No	two

1. My name __is Diego__. __I am__ from Mexico.
   I __was a truck driver__ in Mexico. I ___am___
   married. __There are five__ people in my family.

2. My name _____. _____ from Korea.
   I _____ in Korea. I _____
   married. _____ people in my family.

Check your answers. See page 132.

4 Verb tense review (present and past of regular and irregular verbs)

A Read Henry's journal. Write the correct verb.

We did a lot last weekend! I usually _____ every Saturday, but last

1. work / worked

Saturday, I _____ to a ball game. Sarah usually _____ shopping on

2. go / went   3. goes / went

Saturday, but she _____ to the game with me. We _____ a lot of fun

4. come / came   5. have / had

last Saturday!

Last Sunday, I _____ to work. I _____ last Sunday because

6. go / went   7. work / worked

I _____ to work on Saturday. I usually _____ the bus to work,

8. don't go / didn't go   9. take / took

but last Sunday, I _____ late. I _____ the bus, so I

10. sleep / slept   11. didn't take / don't take

_____ to work!

12. walk / walked

We _____ my parents every weekend, too. We _____ to their house

13. visit / visited   14. go / went

for dinner every Sunday night. But last Sunday, we _____ to a restaurant for

                                                              15. go / went

dinner. We _____ my parents' anniversary last Sunday night. On

16. celebrate / celebrated

Monday morning, I was really tired!

B Fill in the missing words. Use the correct tense.

1. Andy _____*slept*_____ late yesterday.

          (sleep)

2. Mari usually _____ on the weekend.

                  (work)

3. Bill _____ the bus to school every day.

        (take)

4. We _____ our grandparents last week.

        (visit)

5. Anna _____ to school yesterday.

          (walk)

6. Sachi _____ to a ball game last Saturday.

           (go)

7. Jack usually _____ his birthday at a restaurant.

              (celebrate)

8. She _____ _____ anything at the mall yesterday.

        (not)   (buy)

LESSON **A** Listening

1 Look at the picture. Write the words.

| curly hair | long brown hair | short blond hair | striped pants |
| a jogging suit | a long skirt | short brown hair | a white T-shirt |

Alejandro

5. _____

1. _____ *curly hair* _____

2. _____

6. _____

3. _____

7. _____

4. _____

Carlos

8. _____

Jane

Sandra

2 Complete the sentences. Use the words from Exercise 1.

1. Alejandro has _____ *curly hair* _____.

2. Alejandro is wearing _____.

3. Jane has _____.

4. Jane is wearing _____.

5. Carlos has _____.

6. Carlos is wearing _____.

7. Sandra has _____.

8. Sandra is wearing _____.

Check your answers. See page 132.

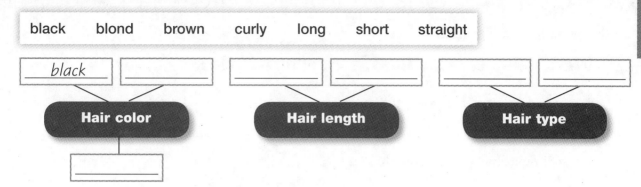

3 Write the words.

| black | blond | brown | curly | long | short | straight |

| _black_ | _____ | | _____ | _____ | | _____ | _____ |

Hair color   **Hair length**   **Hair type**

_____

4 Listen. Circle the correct answers.

TRACK 3

Conversation A

1. James is wearing _____.
   a. extra large pants
   b. a jogging suit
   c. a soccer uniform

2. James has _____.
   a. short curly hair
   b. long hair
   c. short blond hair

Conversation B

3. Lisa is _____.
   a. Miles's wife
   b. James's wife
   c. Miles's daughter

4. Lisa has _____.
   a. long blond hair
   b. short dark hair
   c. short blond hair

Conversation C

5. Sara is _____.
   a. pretty
   b. athletic
   c. tall

6. Sara looks like _____.
   a. Miles
   b. James
   c. Lisa

Check your answers. See page 132.

LESSON B She's wearing a short plaid skirt.

Study the chart on page 131.

1 Write the words in the correct order.

1. striped / a / green and white / dress

   a green and white striped dress

2. shirt / checked / black and blue / a

   _____

3. a / blue / coat / long

   _____

4. small / shoes / white and black

   _____

5. pants / black / plaid

   _____

6. boots / brown / short

   _____

2 Look at the pictures. Write the words from Exercise 1.

1. *a long blue coat*
   _____

2. _____
   _____

3. _____
   _____

4. _____
   _____

5. _____
   _____

6. _____
   _____

Check your answers. See page 132.

3 **Read the sentences. Look at the ad. Circle the correct answers.**

1. Model A is wearing a _____ skirt.
   a. plaid
   b. striped
   c. checked

2. Model A has _____ hair.
   a. long curly
   b. short straight
   c. long straight

3. Model B has _____ hair.
   a. long curly
   b. short curly
   c. short straight

4. Model C is wearing a _____ shirt.
   a. plaid
   b. striped
   c. checked

5. Model D is wearing a striped _____.
   a. sweater
   b. pants
   c. skirt

6. Model E is wearing a long _____.
   a. sweater
   b. coat
   c. dress

4 **Write the words.**

black	green	large	pants	red	small
coat	jeans	long	purple	short	sweater

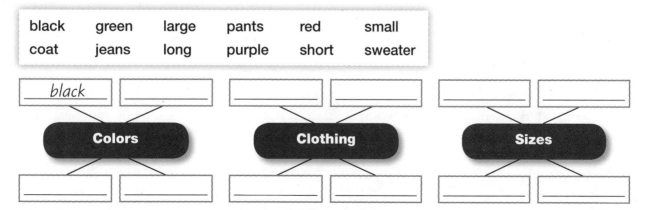

black

Colors   Clothing   Sizes

LESSON C What are you doing right now?

Study the chart on page 126.

1 Read the questions. Circle the answers.

1. What are you doing right now?
   a. I study for a test.
   (b.) I'm studying for a test.

2. What do you usually do at night?
   a. I usually study English.
   b. I am usually studying English.

3. What do you always wear to work?
   a. I'm always wearing my uniform.
   b. I always wear my uniform.

4. What are you wearing today?
   a. I'm wearing jeans and a shirt.
   b. I wear jeans and a shirt.

5. What do you usually do on the weekend?
   a. I visit with my family.
   b. I'm visiting with my family.

6. What do you do every Tuesday?
   a. I'm going to the park.
   b. I go to the park.

2 Complete the conversations. Use the correct form of the verb. Use *am*, *is*, *are*, *do*, or *does*.

1. **A** What _____*do*_____ you _____*do*_____ every Thursday night?
   (do)

   B I _____ English.
   (study)

   A What _____ you _____ now?
   (do)

   B I _____ a book.
   (read)

2. **A** What _____ Jin-ho _____ right now?
   (do)

   B He _____ soccer.
   (play)

   A What _____ Jin-ho usually _____ every day?
   (do)

   B He usually _____ computer games.
   (play)

3. **A** What _____ Ramona _____ every afternoon?
   (do)

   B She _____ .
   (work)

   A What _____ Ramona _____ now?
   (do)

   B She _____ TV.
   (watch)

Check your answers. See page 132.

3 Circle the correct question.

1. He goes home.
   a. What does he do at 9:00?
   b. What is he doing right now?

2. He calls the office.
   a. What does he do every Monday?
   b. What is he doing now?

3. He's watching a movie.
   a. What does he do every night?
   b. What is he doing right now?

4. He's drinking orange juice.
   a. What does he drink every day?
   b. What is he drinking now?

5. He sits at his desk.
   a. Where does he sit every night?
   b. Where is he sitting right now?

6. He's wearing a striped suit.
   a. What does he wear to work every day?
   b. What is he wearing today?

4 Complete the sentences. Use the simple present form of the verbs. Then listen.

TRACK 4

call	go	leave	sit	study	talk

Eduardo usually ___leaves___ English
                      1.
class at 9:00 p.m. He _____ home
                              2.
and _____ his girlfriend, Lisa.
         3.
They usually _____ for 15 minutes.
                    4.
Then Eduardo _____ at his desk.
                      5.
He _____ English late at night.
       6.

5 Complete the sentences. Use the present continuous form of the verbs. Then listen.

TRACK 5

drink	relax	sit	speak	watch	wear

Tonight, Eduardo ___is relaxing___.
                         1.
He _____ TV with Lisa.
         2.
They _____ on the sofa.
           3.
He _____ a soda. He
         4.
_____ jeans and a shirt.
       5.
He _____ English with
         6.
Lisa. She is a good teacher!

Check your answers. See page 133.

LESSON D Reading

TRACK 6

1 Read and complete the chart with the underlined words in the e-mail. Then listen.

From: Mira Hernandez
To: Julia Yee
Date: January 2, 2013 2:06 p.m.
Subject: How are you?

Dear Julia,

I think about you every day. I'm at work right now. I am writing this e-mail in the lunchroom. We miss you here. How is Chicago? We are working very hard. New York is very cold right now. Today I am wearing my jacket, hat, and scarf! The kids both go to school every day. Gabriel wears a uniform to school. It's very cute. Mica goes to a different school. She wears jeans every day.

Please write back!

Lots of love,
Mira

Present continuous	am writing		
Simple present	think		

2 Answer the questions. Use the information from Exercise 1.

1. Where is Mira right now?

   She's in the lunchroom.

2. What city does Julia live in?

   _____

3. What city does Mira live in?

   _____

4. What does Gabriel wear to school?

   _____

5. What does Mica wear to school every day?

   _____

6. What is Mira doing right now?

   _____

Check your answers. See page 133.

3 **Find the words.**

belt	earrings	hat	purse	scarf	tie
bracelet	gloves	necklace	ring	sunglasses	watch

t	f	d	b	a	w	t	o	m	d	e	a
e	t	g	l	o	v	e	s	d	n	a	v
t	n	p	c	b	e	x	u	a	p	r	p
i	z	z	h	a	t	a	n	c	l	r	w
a	n	y	r	d	o	b	g	v	m	i	a
n	t	d	g	m	b	e	l	p	b	n	t
a	p	u	r	s	e	l	a	e	h	g	c
x	v	r	s	k	f	t	s	s	t	s	h
d	v	i	n	t	i	e	s	c	a	r	f
h	b	n	b	r	a	c	e	l	e	t	p
r	a	g	i	k	j	j	s	q	w	w	c
t	n	e	c	k	l	a	c	e	d	d	i

4 **Look at the picture. Write the words from Exercise 3.**

1. _____earrings_____

2. _____

3. _____

4. _____

5. _____

6. _____

7. _____

8. _____

9. _____

10. _____

11. _____

12. _____

Check your answers. See page 133.

UNIT 1

LESSON E Writing

Study the chart on page 131.

1 Read the chart. Complete the paragraphs.

	Sarah	Martina	Norma
Hair color	brown	blond	black
Eye color	brown	blue	green
Clothes	red and white striped sweater, blue jeans	black shirt, black pants, red shoes	blue jacket, yellow shirt, gray plaid skirt
Accessories	scarf, hat	gold watch, red purse	large earrings, rings
After-class activities	go to work	go out with friends	go home
Weekend activities	exercise, play with children	study English, clean house	visit with family, watch children play sports

A

This person has black hair and ____green____ eyes. She _____ home
                                      1.   2.
every day after class. On the weekend, she _____ with her family and
                                                3.
_____ her children play sports. She is wearing a blue _____,
    4.   5.
large _____, and rings. Who is she? _____
         6.   7.

B

This person has _____ eyes and brown hair. She's wearing a red and
                      1.
_____ striped sweater and blue _____. She _____ to
    2.   3.   4.
work after class every day. On the weekend, she exercises and _____
                                                                  5.
with her children. Who is she? _____
                                   6.

C

Today, this person is _____ black clothing. Her _____ and
                          1.   2.
purse are red. She has _____ hair and _____ eyes. After class,
                           3.   4.
she _____ out with her friends. On the weekend, she _____
        5.   6.
English and cleans her house. Who is this person? _____
                                                      7.

Check your answers. See page 133.

2 Rewrite the sentences. Change the underlined words. Use the words in the box.

a backpack	is long	on the weekend
every Monday	is wearing	a watch

1. Bobby goes to New York City every Saturday and Sunday.

   Bobby goes to New York City on the weekend.

2. Georgia is in a black scarf and a red coat.

   _____

3. Susana goes to work after school on Monday.

   _____

4. Mei's hair isn't short.

   _____

5. Martin is carrying his books in a bag on his back.

   _____

6. Christina is wearing a bracelet with a small clock on it.

   _____

3 Rewrite the sentences in a different way.

1. Mary teaches English on the weekend.

   On the weekend, Mary teaches English.

2. Every night, Sam leaves early.

   _____

3. On Thursday, Alberto watches TV.

   _____

4. Raquel plays soccer on Saturday.

   _____

5. Michael wears a suit every Sunday.

   _____

6. Every June, Petra has a birthday party.

   _____

Check your answers. See page 133.

LESSON F Another view

1 **Read the questions. Look at the ad. Fill in the correct answers.**

ALLENE'S ATTIC
ONE-DAY SALE
TODAY ONLY! OPEN 7:00 A.M.-MIDNIGHT!

$14.00
$22.00
$19.99
$95.00
$100.00
$120.00
$62.00
$9.50
$12.00
$25.00
$45.00
$46.50

1. How much does the plaid shirt cost?
   Ⓐ $14.00
   Ⓑ $22.00
   ● $25.00
   Ⓓ $32.00

2. Which item costs $12.00?
   Ⓐ the necklace
   Ⓑ the ring
   Ⓒ the scarf
   Ⓓ the tie

3. When does Allene's Attic close today?
   Ⓐ 7:00 a.m.
   Ⓑ 10:00 a.m.
   Ⓒ noon
   Ⓓ midnight

4. Which item costs $62.00?
   Ⓐ the purse
   Ⓑ the boots
   Ⓒ the coat
   Ⓓ the necklace

5. How much do the pants cost?
   Ⓐ $20.00
   Ⓑ $32.00
   Ⓒ $45.00
   Ⓓ $100.00

6. Which item costs $120.00?
   Ⓐ the tall boots
   Ⓑ the long coat
   Ⓒ the short skirt
   Ⓓ the striped suit

Check your answers. See page 133.

2 Look at the chart. Complete the sentences.

	Rachel	Rob	Dan	Alicia	Luke
Do you wear glasses?	✓		✓		
Do you like sports?		✓		✓	
Do you have a job?	✓	✓			✓
Do you usually eat breakfast?		✓	✓		
Do you watch TV every night?	✓		✓		✓
Do you wear a scarf?				✓	
Do you wear a hat?	✓				
Do you usually wear a watch?		✓		✓	✓

1. Rachel wears glasses, _____ *and Dan does, too* _____.
   (Dan)

2. Luke doesn't wear a hat, _____.
   (Rob)

3. Alicia likes sports, _____.
   (Rachel)

4. Luke has a job, _____.
   (Rob)

5. Rob doesn't wear a scarf, _____.
   (Luke)

6. Dan usually eats breakfast, _____.
   (Alicia)

7. Alicia wears a watch, _____.
   (Luke)

8. Rob doesn't watch TV every night, _____.
   (Alicia)

9. Alicia likes sports, _____.
   (Dan)

10. Dan doesn't wear a watch, _____.
    (Rachel)

Check your answers. See page 133.

LESSON **A** Listening

1 **Write the words.**

a computer lab	a keyboard	a monitor	a student
a hall	a lab instructor	a mouse	

1. _a computer lab_

2. _____

3. _____

4. _____

5. _____

6. _____

7. _____

2 **Complete the conversation.**

computer	instructor	keyboarding	register	skill	work

A Hi. I need to learn _____*keyboarding*_____ .
   1.

B Great. I'm Ms. Moreno. I'm the _____ . Why do you
                                        2.
   want to learn to use a _____ ?
                            3.

A I need to learn for my _____ .
                              4.

B That's great. Keyboarding is an important _____ .
                                                   5.
   Did you _____ in the office?
              6.

A Yes.

B OK. Have a seat, please.

Check your answers. See page 133.

3 Read Diego's schedule. Answer the questions.

Name: *Diego Sanchez*
Student ID: *555-23-0967*

Class	Room	Day	Time	Teacher
English	H102	MW	6:00–7:50 p.m.	Hilary Bowman
Computer lab	H315	MW	8:00–9:50 p.m.	Jane Moreno

1. Who is Ms. Bowman? *Diego's English teacher.* _____

2. Who is Ms. Moreno? _____

3. What is Diego's student ID number? _____

4. Where is the English class? _____

5. When is the English class? _____

6. What class is in room H315? _____

4 Listen. Circle T (True) or F (False).

TRACK 7

GUNDER COLLEGE COMPUTER LAB

Learn on the most up-to-date computers!

Come to room **C23-25** and study with lab instructor **Mr. Lucas.**

Learn about keyboarding, word processing, e-mailing, and using the Internet.

Classes are **MWF 10:00 a.m.–12 noon**
Register in **Room S210.**

Registration hours:
Mon.–Thurs. 8:00 a.m.–8:00 p.m.
and Friday 8:00 a.m.–2:00 p.m. Register by 9/23.

Conversation A

1. Malik and Jenn are in a computer class.   T   (F)

2. Malik wants to register for a computer class.   (T)   F

3. Ms. Grant helped Jenn find an English class.   T   (F)

Conversation B

4. Malik needs to learn computers for his job.   T   (F)

5. Ms. Grant is the computer lab instructor.   T   (F)

6. The computer lab is near the library.   (T)   F

Conversation C

7. Malik doesn't want to learn keyboarding.   (T)   F

8. Computer classes are in the morning.   (T)   F

9. Malik will come to class on Thursday.   T   (F)

LESSON B What do you want to do?

Study the chart on page 127.

1 Match the wants and needs.

1. Lynn wants to fix cars. _f_

2. Joe wants to finish high school. ____

3. I want to get a driver's license. ____

4. Li and Matt want to become citizens. ____

5. Ann wants to make more money. ____

6. Karl wants to learn keyboarding. ____

a. He needs to take a computer class.

b. They need to take a citizenship class.

c. She needs to get a second job.

d. I need to take driving lessons.

e. He needs to take a GED class.

f. She needs to study auto mechanics.

2 Complete the sentences.

1. **A** Maria wants to get a driver's license.

   B She ___*needs to take*___ driving lessons.
   (need / take)

2. **A** What does Jim want to do next year?

   B He _____ to community college.
   (want / go)

3. **A** What does Carrie want to do this year?

   B She _____ a second job.
   (want / get)

4. **A** What do you want to do this afternoon?

   B I _____ to a counselor about the GED.
   (want / talk)

5. **A** Excuse me. Do you need help?

   B Yes, thanks. I _____ keyboarding skills.
   (need / learn)

6. **A** Can I help you?

   B Yes, thank you. I _____ for a citizenship class.
   (need / register)

Check your answers. See page 133.

3 Read the catalog and answer the questions. Then listen.

TRACK 8

Riverdale Adult Classes

Do you want to fix cars?
Auto mechanics: Mon. – Thurs.
8:00 a.m. – 2:00 p.m.
Room 131

Do you want to become a citizen?
Citizenship: Mon. – Thurs.
6:00 p.m. – 9:00 p.m.
Room 220

Do you need to get a driver's license?
Driver education: Mon. – Fri.
2:00 p.m. – 4:00 p.m. by appointment
Outside in the parking lot

Do you need to learn computer skills?
Computer technology: Mon. & Wed.
9:00 a.m. – 11:00 a.m. or
Tues. & Thurs. 1:00 p.m. – 3:00 p.m.
In the computer lab

Do you want to go to college? See our counselors in Room 231.

1. **A** Carlos wants to fix cars. What class does he need to take?

   B *He needs to take an auto mechanics class.*_____

2. **A** My mother needs to get a driver's license. What class does she need to take?

   B _____

3. **A** My wife and I want to become citizens. What class do we need to take?

   B _____

4. **A** Arthur is taking an auto mechanics class. What room does he need to go to?

   B _____

5. **A** You want to go to college. What room do you need to go to?

   B _____

6. **A** My sisters want to learn computer skills. What class do they need to take?

   B _____

Check your answers. See page 133.   UNIT 2   **21**

LESSON C What will you do?

Study the chart on page 129.

1 Complete the sentences. Use *will* or *won't*.

1. Javier needs to get a driver's license. He ___will___ take driving lessons next month.

2. Sally wants to make more money. She _____ take a vocational course.

3. Abram wants to be an auto mechanic. He _____ take a citizenship class.

4. Amelia needs to learn a new language. She _____ register for a class next week.

5. Min has a test tomorrow. She _____ go to the party tonight.

6. Micah needs to open a business. He _____ start business school soon.

2 Read James's calendar. Answer the questions.

James's Calendar

Monday	Tuesday	Wednesday	Thursday	Friday	Saturday	Sunday
take an English class	take a driving lesson	take an English class	work	work	meet Lisa for lunch	call Mom

1. What will James do on Thursday?

   He'll work on Thursday.

2. What will he do on Tuesday?

   _____

3. What will he do on Friday?

   _____

4. What will he do on Saturday?

   _____

5. What will he do on Sunday?

   _____

6. What will he do on Monday and Wednesday?

   _____

Check your answers. See pages 133–134.

3 Look at the pictures. Complete the sentences.

Suk-jin's Plan

This year: go to the U.S.

Next year: study English

In two years: get a GED

In three years: take a
vocational course

In four years: open a business

In five years: buy a house

1. **A** What will Suk-jin do in five years?

   B He'll probably _buy a house_____.

2. **A** What will he do this year?

   B He'll probably _____.

3. **A** What will he do in four years?

   B He'll probably _____.

4. **A** What will he do next year?

   B Maybe he'll _____.

5. **A** What will he do in two years?

   B He'll probably _____.

6. **A** What will he do in three years?

   B He'll probably _____.

4 Write questions.

1. What / she / in five years _What will she do in five years?_____

2. What / he / next year _____

3. What / you / tomorrow _____

4. What / they / this weekend _____

Check your answers. See page 134.

LESSON D Reading

1 **Read and answer the questions about the ad. Then listen.**

Learn Computer Technology at City College

Get a job as a computer technician in 18 months! No time? Don't worry. All courses are at night and on weekends.

There will be an information session on March 14 at 7:30 at City College.

We'll talk about registration, the classes, and the certificate. Come and ask questions! Teachers and current students will be there.

1. How long is the Computer Technology program? _18 months._____

2. When is the information session? _____

3. Where is the information session? _____

4. What will they discuss at the information session? _____

   _____

5. Who will be there from the school? _____

2 **Read about Megan's goal. Circle the correct answers.**

My Goal

I want to open my own coffee shop. I need to take three steps. First, I need to take business classes. Second, I need to get a job in a coffee shop. Third, I need to learn about the coffee-shop business. I think I can reach my goal in three years.

1. Megan wants to _____.
   a. become a citizen
   (b.) open a coffee shop
   c. finish high school

2. First, she needs to _____.
   a. get her GED
   b. get a job
   c. take business classes

3. Second, she needs to _____.
   a. learn about the coffee-shop business
   b. open her coffee shop
   c. get a job in a coffee shop

4. In three years, Megan will probably _____.
   a. open her coffee shop
   b. get a job in a dress shop
   c. finish business school

Check your answers. See page 134.

3 Match the names of the vocational courses.

1. computer __e__
2. criminal ____
3. fitness ____
4. home health ____
5. veterinary ____

a. training
b. care
c. assisting
d. justice
e. networking

4 Look at the pictures. Write the vocational courses.

| computer networking | criminal justice | fitness training | nail care |
| counseling | dental assisting | home health care | veterinary assisting |

Study at Peterson Vocational School!

We offer:

1. _computer networking_
2. _____
3. _____
4. _____

5. _____
6. _____
7. _____
8. _____

Check your answers. See page 134.

LESSON E Writing

1 Match the goals with the steps.

Goals

1. Pablo wants to finish high school. _b_
2. Elena wants to learn keyboarding. ____
3. Jeff wants to learn how to fix cars. ____
4. They want to study criminal justice. ____
5. Marina wants to become a citizen. ____
6. Toan wants to speak and understand English. ____

Steps needed to reach the goals

a. They need to take criminal justice classes.
b. He needs to take the GED test.
c. She needs to take a citizenship class.
d. She needs to take a computer class.
e. He needs to make English-speaking friends.
f. He needs to take an automotive repair class.

2 Read and complete the sentences. Then listen.

TRACK 10

My Goal for Next Year

I have a new goal for next year. I want to get a second job on the weekend. I need to make more money because we have a new baby. I will take three steps to reach my goal. First, I need to talk to people about job possibilities. Second, I need to look for jobs in the newspaper. Third, I need to look for jobs online. I will probably reach my goal in two months.

1. Quan wants to _get a second job on the weekend._____ .
2. He needs more money because _____ .
3. First, he needs to _____ .
4. Second, he needs to _____ .
5. Third, he needs to _____ .
6. He will probably reach his goal in _____ .

Check your answers. See page 134.

3 Complete the sentences.

children   First   goal   Second   Third   year

Rachel's Goal

Rachel has a big ___goal___. She wants
               1.
to help her _____ with their homework.
          2.
_____, she needs to find an adult school.
   3.
_____, she needs to practice her English
   4.
every day. _____, she needs to volunteer
         5.
with the Parent-Teacher Association (PTA) at

her children's school. She'll probably be ready to

help her children next _____.
          6.

4 Answer the questions. Use the story in Exercise 3.

1. What is Rachel's goal?

   She wants to help her children with their homework.

2. What does Rachel need to do first?

   _____

3. What does Rachel need to do second?

   _____

4. What does Rachel need to do third?

   _____

5. When will Rachel be ready to help her children?

   _____

LESSON F Another view

1 **Read the questions. Look at the college catalog. Fill in the correct answers.**

ORANGE COUNTY COMMUNITY COLLEGE

Catalog Page	Courses	Spring	Summer	Fall
51	Criminal Justice	📖		
52	Home Health Care	🏠	📖	
52	Fitness Training	🏠		📖
53	Counseling 1		🏠	📖
54	Veterinary Assisting	🏠		🏠

📖 City Downtown Library   🏠 City Community Center

1. The classes meet in ____.
   Ⓐ one place
   ● two places
   Ⓒ three places
   Ⓓ four places

2. There will be only two courses in the ____.
   Ⓐ fall
   Ⓑ winter
   Ⓒ spring
   Ⓓ summer

3. Classes in ____ are only at the City Downtown Library.
   Ⓐ Criminal Justice
   Ⓑ Veterinary Assisting
   Ⓒ Counseling 1
   Ⓓ Home Health Care

4. Counseling 1 is on catalog page ____.
   Ⓐ 51
   Ⓑ 52
   Ⓒ 53
   Ⓓ 54

5. Students can take ____ in the summer.
   Ⓐ Criminal Justice
   Ⓑ Fitness Training
   Ⓒ Veterinary Assisting
   Ⓓ Home Health Care

6. There will be ____ classes in Veterinary Assisting.
   Ⓐ one
   Ⓑ two
   Ⓒ three
   Ⓓ four

Check your answers. See page 134.

2 Complete the conversation. Write the answers.

1. **A** What are you going to do after class?

   B study / at the library *I'm going to study at the library.*

2. **A** What are you having for dinner tonight?

   B have / chicken _____.

3. **A** What are you going to do this evening?

   B watch / TV _____.

4. **A** When will you get up tomorrow?

   B get up / at 6:00 a.m. _____.

5. **A** What are you doing tomorrow?

   B register / for a class _____.

6. **A** What classes will you take next year?

   B take / Criminal Justice 2 _____.

7. **A** What are you doing this weekend?

   B visit / friends _____.

8. **A** What will you do on your vacation?

   B swim / hike _____.

9. **A** What are you going to do after graduation?

   B get a job _____.

10. **A** What are you taking to the party?

    B take / flowers _____.

Check your answers. See page 134.

3 Friends and family

LESSON A Listening

1 **Complete the words.**

1. s m _o_ k _e_
2. g r ___ c ___ r ___ ___ s
3. b r ___ k ___ n - d ___ w n c ___ r
4. ___ v ___ r h ___ ___ t e d e ___ ___ i n ___

5. w ___ r r ___ e d m ___ n
6. t r ___ n k
7. ___ o o ___

2 **Write the words from Exercise 1.**

1. _____

2. _____

3. _____

4. _____

5. _____

6. _____

7. _____

Check your answers. See page 134.

3 Listen. Complete the conversation.

TRACK 11

A Hi, Miguel.

B Laurie? Are you OK? You sound _____worried_____.
                                              1.

A I'm OK, but the car _____ down.
                               2.

B Where are you?

A We're near the supermarket. I bought a lot of _____. I put them in the
                                                           3.

_____. Then I started the car, but _____ came from
      4.   5.

the _____.
        6.

B Did you open the _____?
                            7.

A Yes. I called the mechanic, too.

B OK. I'll be right there.

LESSON B What did you do last weekend?

Study the chart on page 128.

1 Look at the picture and read the e-mail. Circle the answers.

From: shin17@cup.org
To: grandma17@cup.org
Date: August 10, 2013
Subject: Picnic last week

Here's a picture from last weekend! We had a great time.

Love,
Shin

1. What did Shin do last weekend?
   a. He went to the beach.
   b. He went to the park.

2. Did he take his children?
   a. Yes, he did.
   b. No, he didn't.

3. Did he take the bus?
   a. Yes, he did.
   b. No, he didn't.

4. Did he grill hamburgers?
   a. Yes, he did.
   b. No, he didn't.

5. What did his son do?
   a. He read a book.
   b. He listened to music.

6. Did his daughter listen to music?
   a. Yes, she did.
   b. No, she didn't.

2 Write the simple past.

1. grill _____grilled_____
2. buy _____
3. drive _____
4. eat _____
5. fix _____
6. go _____

7. have _____
8. watch _____
9. meet _____
10. play _____
11. read _____
12. stay _____

Check your answers. See page 134.

3 Complete the sentences. Use the simple past.

1. Frankie and Claudia _____went_____ to the park.
   (go)

2. They _____ their friends.
   (meet)

3. They _____ soccer.
   (play)

4. They _____ a picnic dinner.
   (have)

5. They _____ birthday cake.
   (eat)

6. They _____ home.
   (drive)

4 Match the pictures with the sentences in Exercise 3.

a. _5_

b. _4_

c. _3_

d. _2_

e. _1_

f. _6_

Check your answers. See page 134.

Study the chart on pages 126 and 128.

1 **Complete the sentences. Use the simple present or the simple past.**

1. Anton _____ *went* _____ to English class at 7:00 last night.
   (go)

2. I usually _____ movies on my computer after work.
   (watch)

3. Anita _____ her apartment last Saturday.
   (clean)

4. Tom usually _____ dinner at home.
   (eat)

5. I usually _____ for work at 8:15 a.m.
   (leave)

6. Adriana _____ her friends after class yesterday.
   (meet)

2 **Read Malik's datebook from last week. Match the questions with the answers.**

Sunday	*get up late!*
Monday	*work → 5:00* ~~*tennis with Geraldo 6:00 p.m.*~~
Tuesday	*8:00 ESL class before work* *work → 5:00*
Wednesday	*work → 5:00* *Reza's soccer game 5:30*
Thursday	*8:00 ESL class* *work → 5:00* *birthday dinner at Mom and Dad's at 7:00*
Friday	*leave work early* *citizenship class at 4:00*
Saturday	*tennis with Geraldo 9:00 a.m.*

1. When does Malik usually finish work? __*d*__   a. Tuesday and Thursday.

2. What day did Malik finish work early last week? ____   b. On Sunday.

3. What did Malik have at 4:00 on Friday? ____   c. At his parents' house.

4. When did Malik sleep late? ____   d. At 5:00.

5. Did Malik play tennis with Geraldo on Monday? ____   e. A citizenship class.

6. Where did Malik eat dinner last Thursday? ____   f. No, he didn't.

7. What days does Malik have ESL class? ____   g. On Friday.

8. What day did Malik watch Reza's soccer game? ____   h. On Wednesday.

Check your answers. See page 134.

3 Complete the sentences. Use the simple present or the simple past.

1. Malik _____has_____ an ESL class on Tuesday and Thursday.
   (have)

2. Malik usually _____ tennis with Geraldo on Monday and Saturday.
   (play)

3. Malik _____ until 7:00 last Tuesday.
   (work)

4. Malik _____ a citizenship class every Friday at 4:00.
   (have)

5. Malik and Geraldo _____ for tennis at 9:00 last Saturday morning.
   (meet)

6. Malik usually _____ up late on Sunday.
   (get)

7. Malik and his wife and children usually _____ dinner at home.
   (eat)

8. They _____ dinner at his parents' house last Thursday.
   (eat)

4 Read the Lopez family's calendar. Answer the questions.

Monday	Tuesday	Wednesday	Thursday	Friday
Melissa – movie with Uncle Jaime	Tony – meet friends after work 6:00	Victor – study for English test	Mom and Dad – buy groceries	Mom – take English exam Tony – meet friends after work 5:30

1. When do Mom and Dad usually buy groceries?

   They usually buy groceries on Thursday.

2. When did Mom take her English exam?

   _____

3. What does Tony usually do after work on Tuesday and Friday?

   _____

4. When did Melissa go to a movie with her uncle?

   _____

5. What time did Tony meet his friends last Friday?

   _____

6. What did Victor do last Wednesday?

   _____

LESSON D Reading

1 **Read and circle the correct answers. Then listen.**

TRACK 12

August 10

 Today was a great day. This morning, the children helped me. Ron did the dishes, Lisa made the beds, and Sonia did the laundry. The children are usually busy on the weekend, and Ed usually works. They don't have time to help me. But not today!
 At noon, Ed made lunch for us. Lunch was delicious. After lunch, I had a great afternoon. First, I took a long bath. Then, I took a long nap. I usually go shopping in the afternoon, but not today. After my nap, I got up and got dressed. Then, I made dinner. After dinner, we all watched a movie on TV. Now it's time for bed. What a great day!

1. Who helped Ana today?
   a. Ron
   b. Lisa
   c. Sonia
   (d.) all of the above

2. Who did the dishes?
   a. Ed
   b. Lisa
   c. Ron
   d. Sonia

3. Who made the beds?
   a. Ed
   b. Lisa
   c. Ron
   d. Sonia

4. Who did the laundry?
   a. Ed
   b. Lisa
   c. Ron
   d. Sonia

5. Who made lunch?
   a. Ed
   b. Lisa
   c. Ron
   d. Sonia

6. Who usually helps Ana?
   a. Ana's friends
   b. the children
   c. Ed
   d. none of the above

7. Who took a long bath and a long nap?
   a. Ana
   b. the children
   c. Ed
   d. all of the above

8. Who made dinner?
   a. Ana
   b. the children
   c. Ed
   d. all of the above

Check your answers. See page 134.

2 Complete the chart.

| a bath | the bed | the dishes | dressed | the laundry | lunch | a nap | up |

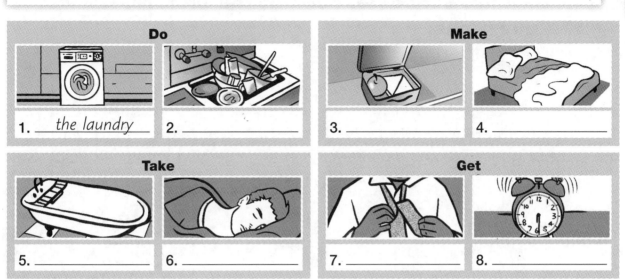

Do

1. _the laundry_   2. _____

Make

3. _____   4. _____

Take

5. _____   6. _____

Get

7. _____   8. _____

3 Read the conversation. Write *do*, *get*, *make*, or *take* in the simple present or simple past. Then listen.

TRACK 13

MOM   Sonia, did you _____*make*_____ the beds this morning?
1.

SONIA   No, I didn't, Mom. I _____ up late today. But I always make the beds.
2.
It's Ron's turn.

RON   Mom, I can't make the beds. I don't have time. And I always _____ the
3.
dishes. It's Lisa's turn.

LISA   OK, Mom. In a minute.

MOM   Ron, did you _____ the dishes this morning?
4.

RON   Yes, I _____.
5.

MOM   And what about your homework?

RON   I _____ my homework yesterday. Today is Saturday.
6.

MOM   OK. Did Dad _____ the laundry this morning?
7.

SONIA   No, Mom. He always _____ a nap on Saturday.
8.

MOM   A nap! It's 9:00 a.m.!

Check your answers. See page 135.

LESSON E Writing

1 **Read Ana's schedule. Look at the picture. Answer the questions.**

Usually

My Morning Schedule
6:00: Get up and take a bath.
6:15: Get Ed up and get dressed.
6:30: Get Sonia up and then make the children's lunches for school.
6:45: Get Ron up and then make my lunch.
7:10: Get Lisa up and then eat my breakfast.
7:15: Make the children's beds.
7:20: Ed leaves for work.
7:30: Children leave for school.
7:45: Do the dishes.
7:55: Leave for work.

This morning

1. Who usually gets up first?

   Ana usually gets up first.

2. Who got up first this morning?

   _____

3. Who usually takes a bath every morning?

   _____

4. Who didn't take a bath this morning?

   _____

5. Who usually leaves for work at 7:20?

   _____

6. Who usually leaves for school at 7:30?

   _____

Check your answers. See page 135.

2 **Answer the questions. Use Ana's schedule in Exercise 1.**

1. When does Ana get up? *She gets up at 6:00.*

2. When does Ana get dressed? _____

3. When does Ana eat her breakfast? _____

4. When does Ana do the dishes? _____

5. When does Ana make the children's beds? _____

   _____

6. When does Ana leave the house? _____

3 **Read the sentences. Write *First*, *Next*, or *Finally* on the correct line.**

1. Last Monday, I had a very bad morning.

   _____N'_____, I didn't have time for breakfast.

   _____First_____, I woke up late.

   _____, I was late for work.

2. Last Sunday, my family went to the beach.

   _____, we drove home for dinner.

   _____, we had a picnic lunch.

   _____, we relaxed all afternoon.

4 **Write the sentences from Exercise 3 in the correct order.**

1. *Last Monday, I had a very bad morning. First, I woke up late. Next,* _____

   _____

   _____

2. _____

   _____

   _____

LESSON F Another view

1 **Read the questions. Look at the ad. Fill in the correct answers.**

JACKSON REPAIR

Next to the supermarket on Washington Street (973) 555-1850

- We fix car problems from hood to trunk!
- SUMMER REPAIR SPECIAL: 20% off!
- ENGINE SPECIAL: $150
- BROKEN-DOWN CAR?
  We'll bring you home! $50

OPEN MONDAY–SATURDAY 8:00 a.m.–6:00 p.m.

1. How much is the Engine Special?
   Ⓐ $50
   Ⓑ $100
   ● $150
   Ⓓ $200

2. What is the Jackson Repair phone number?
   Ⓐ 20%
   Ⓑ $50
   Ⓒ $150
   Ⓓ (973) 555-1850

3. What is the Summer Repair Special?
   Ⓐ 20% off
   Ⓑ $50 off
   Ⓒ 50% off
   Ⓓ $150 off

4. Which days is Jackson Repair open?
   Ⓐ Monday–Friday
   Ⓑ Monday–Saturday
   Ⓒ Monday–Sunday
   Ⓓ Sunday–Saturday

5. When is Jackson Repair open?
   Ⓐ 6:00 a.m.–8:00 p.m.
   Ⓑ 6:00 p.m.–8:00 p.m.
   Ⓒ 8:00 a.m.–6:00 p.m.
   Ⓓ 8:00 p.m.–6:00 a.m.

6. Where is Jackson Repair?
   Ⓐ at home
   Ⓑ on Jackson Street
   Ⓒ in the supermarket
   Ⓓ on Washington Street

Check your answers. See page 135.

2 Complete the story about the Ramirez family's weekend schedule. Use *do*, *make*, *play*, or *go*.

The Ramirez Family's Weekend Schedule			
Grandma Rosa	Jorge & Sara	Lorena	Daniel
• Cookies for the family on Saturday morning • Cards with the Lings on Saturday night • Dinner for the family on Sunday	• Housework on Saturday morning • Dancing at the club on Saturday night • Breakfast for the family on Sunday morning	• Soccer on Saturday morning • Shopping on Saturday afternoon • Homework on Sunday afternoon	• Basketball on Friday night • Chores on Saturday morning • Computer games on Saturday night

The Ramirez family is very busy on the weekend. On Saturday morning, Grandma

Rosa _____makes cookies_____ for the family. On Saturday night, she usually
                 1.

_____ with the Lings. She _____ for the family on
         2.   3.

Sunday. Jorge and Sara _____ on Saturday morning. They usually
                                4.

_____ on Saturday night, and they _____ for the
         5.   6.

family on Sunday morning. On Saturday morning, Lorena _____.
                                                                7.

On Saturday afternoon, she usually _____ for groceries. She
                                            8.

_____ on Sunday afternoon. Daniel _____ on Friday
         9.   10.

night. He _____ on Saturday morning, and he _____
                 11.   12.

on Saturday night.

Check your answers. See page 135.

LESSON **A** Listening

1 Complete the words.

1. i n j u r _e_ d h ___ n d
2. c r ___ t c h ___ s
3. s p r a ___ n ___ d ___ n k l ___
4. b r ___ k ___ n b ___ n ___

5. ___ n h ___ l ___ r
6. X - r ___ ___
7. p ___ i n f ___ l k n ___ ___

2 Look at the picture. Write the words from Exercise 1.

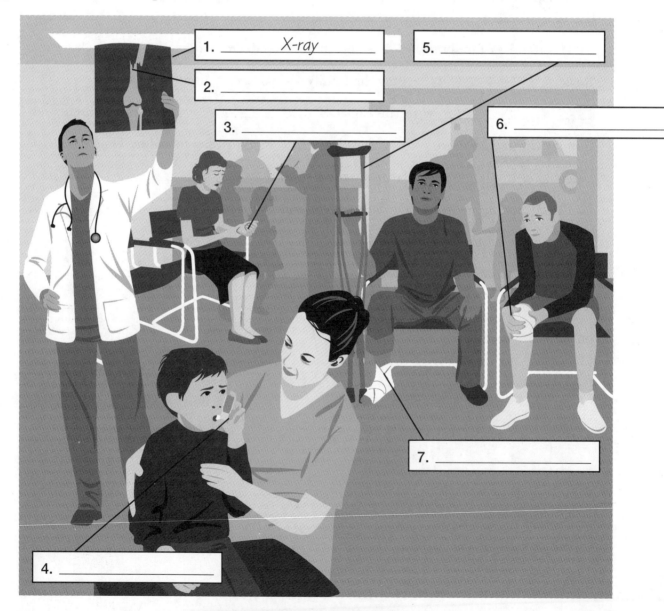

1. _____X-ray_____
2. _____
3. _____
4. _____
5. _____
6. _____
7. _____

Check your answers. See page 135.

3 Complete the story. Use the words from Exercise 1.

It's a busy day at the hospital. A man had an accident at work. He has a ___*sprained*___

1.

ankle. He can't walk. He needs _____ . A woman had an accident, too. Now she

2.

has an _____ hand. The doctor is looking at an _____ . It's a picture of a

3.   4.

_____ bone. The nurse is helping a little boy. She gives him an _____ .

5.   6.

4 Listen. Circle the correct answers.

TRACK 14

Conversation A

1. Who had an accident?
   a. Ricardo
   b. Susanna
   c. the children

2. Where did the accident happen?
   a. at work
   b. at home
   c. at school

3. Where will Susanna go after the phone call?
   a. to the hospital
   b. to work
   c. to school

Conversation B

4. Where is Susanna right now?
   a. at home
   b. at work
   c. at the hospital

5. What happened to Susanna?
   a. She sprained her ankle.
   b. She broke her arm.
   c. She broke her leg.

6. Where is the hospital?
   a. on Pine Street
   b. on 15th Street
   c. on 50th Street

Check your answers. See page 135.

LESSON B You should go to the hospital.

Study the chart on page 129.

1 Circle should or shouldn't.

1. Karl's tooth hurts. He **should** / **shouldn't** go to the dentist.

2. The children are all sick. They **should** / **shouldn't** go to school today.

3. My eyes hurt. I **should** / **shouldn't** watch TV right now.

4. Your leg is very sore. You **should** / **shouldn't** get an X-ray.

5. Mario hurt his back. He **should** / **shouldn't** see a doctor.

6. Alissa has a stomachache. She **should** / **shouldn't** eat a big dinner.

2 Complete the sentences. Use should or shouldn't.

1. *A* Uncle Pete has a bottle of medicine.

   B He ___*shouldn't*___ keep it in a hot place.

   He ___*should*___ keep it away from children.

2. *A* Sue has a headache.

   B She _____ listen to loud music.

   She _____ take some aspirin.

3. *A* Abel has a stomachache.

   B He _____ take some medicine.

   He _____ eat his lunch.

4. *A* Francine has a sprained ankle.

   B She _____ play soccer.

   She _____ get a pair of crutches.

5. *A* I'm very hot. I don't feel well.

   B You _____ drink a lot of water.

   You _____ stay in the sun.

6. *A* Mrs. Lam hurt her leg.

   B She _____ see a doctor.

   She _____ walk.

Check your answers. See page 135.

3 Complete the sentences.

break	shade	towel
clothes	sun	water

You're working outside. It's very hot. What should you do? What shouldn't you do?

✓ You shouldn't wear heavy ___*clothes*___ .
                                       1.

✓ You should take a _____ and drink a lot of _____ .
                              2.   3.

✓ You should use a wet _____ .
                              4.

✓ You shouldn't stay in the _____ . You should stay in the _____ .
                                         5.   6.

4 Complete the sentences. Use *should* or *shouldn't*.

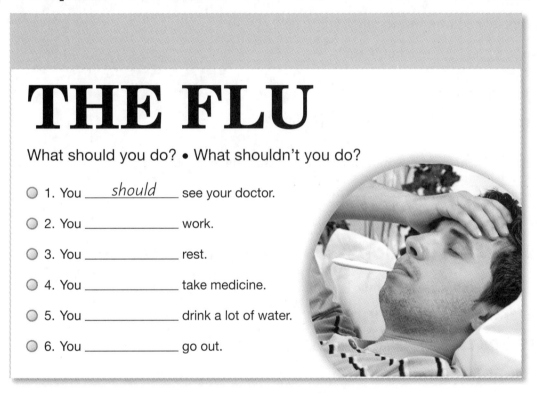

THE FLU

What should you do? • What shouldn't you do?

○ 1. You ___*should*___ see your doctor.

○ 2. You _____ work.

○ 3. You _____ rest.

○ 4. You _____ take medicine.

○ 5. You _____ drink a lot of water.

○ 6. You _____ go out.

Check your answers. See page 135.

LESSON C You have to see a doctor.

Study the chart on page 127.

1 Complete the conversations. Use *have to* or *has to*. Then listen.

TRACK 15

1. **A** Linda hurt her hand. What does she have to do?

   B She ___*has to*___ see a doctor.

2. **A** Rod hurt his back. What does he have to do?

   B He _____ stay home today.

3. **A** Jimmy broke his arm. What do we have to do?

   B We _____ take Jimmy to the hospital.

4. **A** I have a headache. What do I have to do?

   B You _____ go home early.

5. **A** Tim broke his leg. What does he have to do?

   B He _____ use these crutches.

6. **A** Jerry and Charlie have asthma. What do they have to do?

   B They _____ take their medicine.

2 Answer the questions. Use *have to* or *has to*.

1. Jesse sprained his ankle. What does he have to do?

   (use crutches) *He has to use crutches.* _____

2. Mari burned her hand. What does she have to do?

   (see the doctor) _____

3. Irvin broke his arm. What does he have to do?

   (get an X-ray) _____

4. Elian hurt his hand at work. What does he have to do?

   (fill out an accident report) _____

5. Rosa has a headache. What does she have to do?

   (take medicine) _____

Check your answers. See page 135.

3 Match the sentences with the labels.

1. You have to take this in the morning. _c_

2. You have to keep this in the refrigerator. ____

3. You have to eat when you take this. ____

4. You have to use this at night. ____

5. You have to keep this out of the refrigerator. ____

6. You have to use this in your eye. ____

 a FOR THE eye

 b DO NOT Refrigerate

 c TAKE IN THE MORNING

 d TAKE WITH FOOD OR MILK

 e BEDTIME

 f Refrigerate

4 Complete the conversation.

do	food	have to	medicine	morning	prescription	refrigerator

A Here's your _____prescription_____, Mrs. Lopez.
1.

B Thanks. What _____ I have to do?
2.

A You _____ keep this _____ in the _____.
3.   4.   5.

B OK. Can I take it in the _____?
6.

A Yes, and you have to take it with _____.
7.

B I see. I'll take it with my breakfast. Thank you, Dr. Simmons.

Check your answers. See page 135.

LESSON **D** Reading

1 Read and circle the correct answers. Then listen.

TRACK 16

KNOW YOUR BLOOD PRESSURE

Are you over 21? Yes? Your doctor should check your blood pressure every year. High blood pressure can be dangerous. Here are some ways to lower your blood pressure. First, try to change your lifestyle:

- Stop smoking
- Lose weight.
- Exercise every day.
- Eat lots of fruits and vegetables. Don't eat a lot of fat.
- Don't use a lot of salt. Don't drink a lot of coffee.
- Reduce your stress.

Second, talk to your doctor about your blood pressure. Maybe you need to take medicine. Talk to your doctor! Start today!

1. What should you do to lower your blood pressure?
   a. change your lifestyle
   b. drink coffee
   c. eat fat
   d. use salt

2. You have high blood pressure. What should you eat?
   a. fat
   b. fruits
   c. salt
   d. none of the above

3. You need to lower your blood pressure. What should you do?
   a. drink coffee
   b. start smoking
   c. eat healthy foods
   d. use salt

4. You need to change your diet. What should you do?
   a. drink coffee
   b. eat vegetables
   c. exercise
   d. take medicine

5. You need to lose weight. When should you exercise?
   a. every year
   b. every month
   c. every week
   d. every day

6. Who should check your blood pressure?
   a. your doctor
   b. your English teacher
   c. your parents
   d. none of the above

Check your answers. See page 135.

2 Match the words.

1. a swollen _d_
2. high blood ____
3. a sprained ____
4. a stiff ____
5. chest ____

a. neck
b. wrist
c. pains
d. knee
e. pressure

3 Look at the pictures. Write sentences. Use *has* or *have*.

1. ___She has a rash.___

2. _____

3. _____

4. _____

5. _____

6. _____

4 Complete the sentences.

accident	chest	cut	hurt	medicine

- Did someone get ___hurt___?
  1.
- Was there a bad _____?
  2.
- Does someone have _____ pains?
  3.
- Does someone have a bad _____?
  4.
- Did a child take your _____?
  5.

EMERGENCY? CALL 911

Check your answers. See page 135.

LESSON E Writing

1 **Read the questions. Look at the form. Answer the questions.**

Sleepy Burgers: Accident Log   **August 2013**

Employee	Job	Date	Where	Injury
J. Haddan	Server	8-3-13	Dining Room	Sprained ankle
M. Almaleh	Cook	8-10-13	Kitchen	Burned hand
F. Engels	Cook	8-12-13	Kitchen	Cut hand
E. Perry	Hostess	8-20-13	Dining Room	Sprained wrist

Problems? Call the U.S. Department of Labor at (800) 555-0810.

1. How many accidents were there at the restaurant in August?

   There were four accidents in August.

2. Who had a sprained ankle?

   _____

3. When did the cook burn his hand?

   _____

4. What did Mr. Engels cut?

   _____

5. What was Ms. Perry's injury?

   _____

6. What is the name of the restaurant?

   _____

2 **Number the sentences in the correct order.**

1. Yesterday, I cut my hand.
   - ____ The knife slipped.
   - _1_ I was cooking dinner.
   - ____ My hands were wet.

2. Yesterday, I burned my leg.
   - ____ My son ran into the table.
   - ____ I was eating hot soup.
   - ____ The table fell over.

Check your answers. See page 135.

3 Complete the sentences.

accident	days	injuries	shouldn't
burned	has to	medicine	work

Cottage Hospital

Report

I treated Carlos Garcia today, 5/09/2013, for ___burned___
1.
hands. He got these _____ at work at Fast Frank's
2.
Restaurant this afternoon. He says it was an _____.
3.

Recommendations

1. Carlos _____ take one ounce of this _____
4.   5.
every four hours for ten _____.
6.
2. Carlos _____ work for one week. He can return
7.
to _____ on May 16, 2013.
8.

Signature _William Crawford M.D._

Date _May 9, 2013_

4 Answer the questions. Use the report in Exercise 3.

1. Who was hurt?

   Carlos Garcia was hurt.

2. What was his injury?

   _____

3. When was he hurt?

   _____

4. Was it an accident?

   _____

5. When can he return to work?

   _____

6. What is the name of the restaurant?

   _____

LESSON F Another view

1 **Read the questions. Look at the bar graph. Fill in the correct answers.**

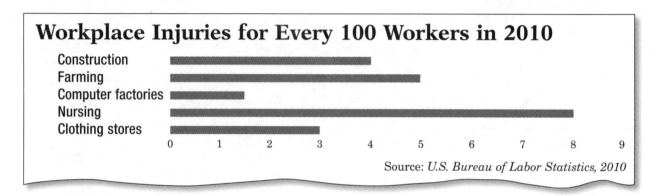

Workplace Injuries for Every 100 Workers in 2010

Construction
Farming
Computer factories
Nursing
Clothing stores

0 1 2 3 4 5 6 7 8 9

Source: *U.S. Bureau of Labor Statistics, 2010*

1. What year is this bar graph for?
   Ⓐ 2000
   Ⓑ 2005
   ● 2010
   Ⓓ 2013

2. For every 100 workers, which workplace had eight injuries?
   Ⓐ construction
   Ⓑ farming
   Ⓒ nursing
   Ⓓ clothing stores

3. For every 100 workers, which workplace had one and a half injuries?
   Ⓐ farming
   Ⓑ nursing
   Ⓒ clothing stores
   Ⓓ computer factories

4. For every 100 workers, how many injuries happened on farms?
   Ⓐ 2
   Ⓑ 3
   Ⓒ 5
   Ⓓ 9

5. For every 100 workers, how many injuries happened in clothing stores?
   Ⓐ 2
   Ⓑ 3
   Ⓒ 6
   Ⓓ 9

6. Which workplace had the most injuries?
   Ⓐ nursing
   Ⓑ clothing stores
   Ⓒ construction
   Ⓓ farming

2 **Complete the sentences.**

| doctor | drowsiness | product | tablets |

1. Do not take more than 8 _____*tablets*_____ in 24 hours.

2. Ask a _____ before use if you have liver or kidney disease.

3. When using this _____, do not take more than directed.

4. This medicine can cause _____.

Check your answers. See page 136.

3 Read the label. Match the words in Column 1 with the words in Column 2. Then complete the sentences with *have to / must, must not,* or *don't have to.*

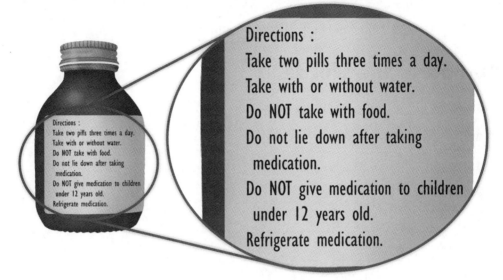

Directions :
Take two pills three times a day.
Take with or without water.
Do NOT take with food.
Do not lie down after taking medication.
Do NOT give medication to children under 12 years old.
Refrigerate medication.

Column 1

1. have to / must

2. must not

3. don't have to

Column 2

a. take the pills three times a day

b. refrigerate this medication

c. give this medication to an eight-year-old.

d. take six pills a day.

e. lie down after you take this medication

f. take this medication with water

1. You _____*have to / must*_____ take the pills three times a day.

2. You _____ refrigerate this medication.

3. You _____ give this medication to an eight-year-old.

4. You _____ take six pills a day.

5. You _____ lie down after you take this medication.

6. You _____ take this medication with water.

Check your answers. See page 136. **UNIT 4 53**

LESSON **A** Listening

1 **Complete the words.**

1. a s <u>u</u> <u>i</u> t c <u>a</u> s <u>e</u>

2. an ____ n f ____ r m ____ t ____ ____ n d ____ s k

3. a w ____ ____ t ____ n g ____ r ____ ____

4. a t r ____ c k

5. a t ____ c k ____ t b ____ ____ t h

6. d ____ p ____ r t ____ r ____ s

7. a r r ____ v ____ l s

2 **Look at the picture. Write the words from Exercise 1.**

1. _____a ticket booth_____

4. _____

2. _____

5. _____

6. _____

3. _____

7. _____

Check your answers. See page 136.

3 Match the actions with the pictures.

a.  TICKETS

b.

c.  INFORMATION

d.  TRACK 5

e.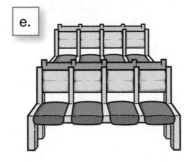

f.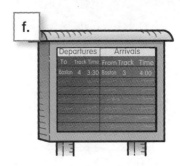

b 1. You put your clothes in this.

____ 2. Your train leaves from here.

____ 3. You look for train times here.

____ 4. You ask questions here.

____ 5. You buy your ticket here.

____ 6. You can sit here to wait for your train.

4 Listen. Circle T (True) or F (False).

TRACK 17

Conversation A

1. The next train for Philadelphia will leave at 5:20.	T	(F)
2. Oscar and Lily need to get train information.	T	F
3. The information booth is next to Track 1.	T	F

Conversation B

4. Trains leave for Philadelphia every half hour.	T	F
5. Oscar and Lily will take the 10:20 train.	T	F
6. The 10:20 train leaves from Track 5.	T	F

Conversation C

7. Two tickets to Philadelphia cost $100.	T	F
8. It takes an hour and 30 minutes to get to Philadelphia on the 10:20 train.	T	F
9. Oscar usually goes to Philadelphia by train.	T	F

Check your answers. See page 136. **UNIT 5 55**

LESSON B How often? How long?

1 **Read the questions. Look at the train schedule. Circle the correct answers.**

Los Angeles Unity Station
Pacific Express – San Diego to Los Angeles

MONDAY THROUGH FRIDAY

Departs San Diego	Arrives Los Angeles	Duration
12:10 p.m.	2:55 p.m.	2 H 45 M
3:10 p.m.	5:55 p.m.	2 H 45 M
6:10 p.m.	9:10 p.m.	3 H
9:10 p.m.	1:25 a.m.	4 H 14 M

SATURDAY AND SUNDAY

6:45 a.m.	9:45 a.m.	3 H
2:26 p.m.	4:26 p.m.	2 H
6:10 p.m.	9:35 p.m.	3 H 25 M

1. How often does the train go from San Diego to Los Angeles
   on the weekend?
   a. three times a day
   b. four times a day
   c. ten times a day

2. How long does it take to go from San Diego to Los Angeles
   on the 3:10 p.m. train?
   a. two hours and 45 minutes
   b. three hours
   c. four hours and 10 minutes

3. How often does the train go from San Diego to Los Angeles
   on weekdays?
   a. three times a day
   b. four times a day
   c. seven times a day

4. How long does it take to go from San Diego to Los Angeles
   on the 6:45 a.m. train on the weekend?
   a. two hours
   b. two hours and 25 minutes
   c. three hours

Check your answers. See page 136.

2 Match the questions with the answers. Use the schedule in Exercise 1.

1. How often do trains go from San Diego to Los Angeles on weekdays? __f__

2. How long does it take to go to Los Angeles on the 9:10 p.m. train? ____

3. How often do you take the train to Los Angeles? ____

4. How long does it take to drive from San Diego to Los Angeles? ____

5. How often do the trains go to Los Angeles on the weekend? ____

6. How long does it take to go to Los Angeles on the Saturday afternoon train? ____

a. It takes four hours and 15 minutes.

b. I take the train there once or twice a month.

c. It takes two hours.

d. They go to Los Angeles three times a day.

e. It takes a long time to drive there.

f. They go every three hours.

3 Read the chart and write the questions. Then listen.

TRACK 18

	How often?	How long?
drive to the beach	twice a month	one hour
walk to the park	three or four times a week	half an hour
go downtown by bus	every day	45 minutes

1. **A** _How often do you drive to the beach?_ _____

   B Twice a month.

   A _How long does it take?_ _____

   B About one hour.

2. **A** _____

   B About three or four times a week.

   A _____

   B About half an hour.

3. **A** _____

   B Every day.

   A _____

   B About 45 minutes.

LESSON C She often walks to school.

1 **Put the words in order by frequency.**

| always | never | often | rarely | sometimes |

0% ←————————————————————————→ 100%

1. ___never___   2. _____   3. _____   4. _____   5. _____

2 **Read the chart. Complete the sentences. Use the words from Exercise 1.**

English 201	September – October	Number of classes: 45
Name	Number of times late	
Wang-jie	40	
Ayuko	37	
Diana	0	
Arturo	3	
Marisol	45	
Pedro	20	

1. Ayuko is _____often_____ late for class.

2. Ayuko _____ arrives on time.

3. Marisol is _____ late for class.

4. Marisol _____ arrives on time.

5. Diana is _____ on time for class.

6. Diana _____ arrives late.

7. Pedro is _____ late for class.

8. Pedro _____ arrives on time.

9. Arturo _____ arrives late.

10. Arturo is _____ on time.

11. Wang-jie is _____ late.

12. Wang-jie _____ arrives on time.

Check your answers. See page 136.

3 Read the chart. Answer the questions.

Edwin	Never	Rarely	Usually	Always
walks to school				✓
drives to school	✓			
eats lunch at 1:00 p.m.		✓		
eats dinner at home			✓	
goes to sleep at 10:00 p.m.			✓	

1. **A** How often does Edwin walk to school?

   B *He always walks to school.*

2. **A** How often does Edwin drive to school?

   B _____

3. **A** How often does Edwin eat lunch at 1:00 p.m.?

   B _____

4. **A** How often does Edwin eat dinner at home?

   B _____

5. **A** How often does Edwin go to sleep at 10:00 p.m.?

   B _____

4 Read the sentences. Circle *Yes* or *No*.

1. Linda goes out to a restaurant about twice a year.

   a. Linda rarely goes out to a restaurant.   (Yes) No
   b. Linda always eats at home.   Yes No

2. Fred's car is very old. It often breaks down. Fred takes the bus to work when his car is broken down. He drives his car to work when it is fixed.

   a. Fred never drives to work.   Yes No
   b. Fred often takes the bus.   Yes No

3. Our favorite lunch place is Sam's Sandwich Shop. We go there about three times a week. On the other days, we bring our lunch from home.

   a. We always eat lunch out.   Yes No
   b. We sometimes bring our lunch.   Yes No

Check your answers. See page 136.

LESSON **D** Reading

1 **Read and circle the correct answers. Then listen.**

TRACK 19

> Dear Nina,
>
>   We're having a wonderful time in Miami. We
> always have a lot of fun here. We usually stay with
> Mariam's relatives, but they're not here right now.
> This time we're staying at a hotel. We usually come
> to Miami two or three times a year. Layla always
> wants to go shopping at Miami International
> Mall. She likes to buy souvenirs there. Ali never
> wants to go shopping. He wants to go swimming.
> Mariam and I like to go sightseeing, but the
> children rarely go with us. I always take a lot of
> pictures. We'll show you our pictures next week!
>
> Love from us,
>
> Khalid

1. Khalid and his family ____ go to Miami.
   a. never
   b. rarely
   c. often
   d. always

2. ____ always wants to go shopping.
   a. Ali
   b. Khalid
   c. Layla
   d. Mariam

3. Khalid always ____.
   a. goes shopping
   b. goes sightseeing
   c. goes swimming
   d. takes a lot of pictures

4. Khalid and Mariam rarely ____.
   a. go sightseeing together
   b. go sightseeing with the children
   c. stay with Mariam's relatives
   d. take pictures

2 **Circle the answers. Use the information in Exercise 1.**

1. The name of Khalid's wife is **Mariam** / **Layla**.

2. Khalid and his family are staying **with relatives** / **at a hotel**.

3. Khalid and his family **know** / **don't know** Miami very well.

4. Khalid and **Layla** / **Mariam** go sightseeing together.

Check your answers. See page 136.

3 Complete the sentences. Use the correct form of the verbs in the box.

buy	go	stay	take	write

1. Lee usually _____*goes*_____ swimming on Saturday afternoon.

2. Ralph sometimes _____ with relatives in San Francisco.

3. Jon always _____ pictures when he's on vacation.

4. Do you like to _____ sightseeing in a new place?

5. My son rarely wants to _____ shopping with me.

6. I often _____ souvenirs when I'm on vacation.

7. How many suitcases do you usually _____ with you?

8. Don't forget to _____ postcards to me from New York City.

9. Marco sometimes _____ at a hotel when he travels.

4 Number the sentences in the correct order. Then write the conversation below.

_____ It usually takes about three hours by plane.

_____ Where do you usually go?

_____ I go on vacation once a year.

_____ Oh, yes! It takes two days by car.

_____ How long does it take to get there?

__1_ How often do you go on vacation?

_____ Do you always go by plane?

_____ I usually go to Denver to see my parents.

A *How often do you go on vacation?* _____

B _____

A _____

B _____

A _____

B _____

A _____

B _____

Check your answers. See page 136.

LESSON E Writing

1 Write the questions.

1. go to / Miami / How often / trains / do / ?

   How often do trains go to Miami?

2. does / it / San Francisco / How long / take / to get to / ?

   _____

3. to drive to / take / does / it / Detroit / How long / ?

   _____

4. go to / does / the bus / How often / Boston / ?

   _____

5. do / you / your relatives / visit / How often / in Houston / ?

   _____

6. do / stay / you / Where / usually / ?

   _____

2 Write the number of the question from Exercise 1 next to the correct answer.

a. Once or twice a year. ___5___   d. We always stay with my relatives. _____

b. They go every hour. _____   e. It takes about seven hours. _____

c. It goes three times a day. _____   f. It takes about two hours by car. _____

3 Write the durations.

Start	Stop	
12:00	1:05	1. *one hour and five minutes*
8:00	9:45	2.
9:00	9:09	3.
4:00	5:07	4.
4:30	5:00	5.
6:00	7:12	6.

Check your answers. See page 136.

4 Read and answer the questions. Then listen.

TRACK 20

Liz's Life

Liz lives in San Antonio, Texas. Every year, Liz goes to Denver to see her mother and father. She usually stays in Denver for about a week. Liz misses her parents. She rarely has time off from work to visit them. But Liz has a very good job in San Antonio. She works as a receptionist in a printing company. She is very happy there.

1. How often does Liz visit her parents? _____

2. How long does she usually stay in Denver? _____

3. How often does Liz have time off from work? _____

4. How does Liz feel about her job in San Antonio? _____

5 Complete the story.

Martin usually _____*goes*_____ to work by
                    1. go
train. It _____ about 30 minutes to
            2. take
get to work by train. Martin _____ his
                                3. leave
house at 7:15 a.m. He usually _____ to
                                4. get
work at 8:00. He _____ to be late for
                  5. not like
work. Sometimes the trains _____ late.
                            6. be
Martin _____ his laptop computer on
        7. use
the train. He rarely _____ on the train
                      8. sleep
in the morning. Sometimes he _____ a
                                9. take
nap on the trip home. He never _____
                                10. talk
to people on the train. Martin _____
                                11. like
the train. He _____ to drive to work.
            12. not like

Check your answers. See page 136.

LESSON F Another view

1 Write the question. Find the answer in the chart. Then write the answer.

How Students Get to School Each Morning

Name	Transportation	Why	Duration	Arrival at school
Mai		• Goes every half hour • Cheap	• 10 minutes to bus stop • 10 minutes on bus	• Usually 10 minutes early • Sometimes late
Shen-hui		• No waiting • Good exercise	• 20 minutes	• Always on time
Phillipe		• No waiting • Good exercise	• 35 minutes	• Always on time
Sara		• Goes every 5 minutes • Usually on time	• 15 minutes to subway • 7 minutes on subway	• Rarely late
Zoe		• No waiting	• 7 minutes in car • 2–15 minutes to park car	• Often 5 minutes late

1. How often / bus / go _How often does the bus go?_____
   _It goes every half hour._____

2. How / Shen-hui / get to school _____
   _____

3. How long / to get / from Shen-hui's house / to school / by bicycle _____
   _____

4. How often / Phillipe / arrive on time _____
   _____

5. How long / to get / from Sara's house / to school / by subway _____
   _____

6. How / Zoe / get to school _____
   _____

Check your answers. See page 137.

2 Look at the map. Complete the directions. Circle and write the correct word.

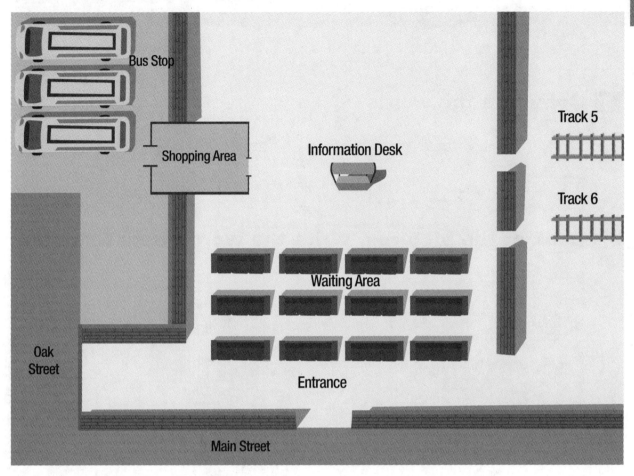

1. You are on Main Street and want to go to the bus stop.

Walk _____ the train station from Main Street. Go
　　　　　　1. out of / into

_____ the waiting area. Walk _____ the
　　2. through / out of　　　　　　　　　　3. into / toward

information desk. Turn left. Then walk _____ the shopping area. Go
　　　　　　　　　　　　　　　　4. into / out of

_____ the shopping area. When you come _____ the
　　5. toward / through　　　　　　　　　　　　　　6. into / out of

shopping area, turn right. The bus stop will be on your right.

2. Your train just arrived at Track 5. You want to go to Oak Street.

Walk _____ the train to Track 5. Walk _____
　　　　7. into / out of　　　　　　　　　　　8. toward / through

the door for track five. Walk _____ the Information Desk. Walk
　　　　　　　　　　　　　9. toward / through

_____ the waiting area. Go _____ the entrance on Main
　　10. into / out of　　　　　　　　　　11. into / out of

Street. Turn right and walk about a block. You'll be at Oak Street.

Check your answers. See page 137.　　　　UNIT 5 **65**

LESSON **A** Listening

1 **Complete the words**

1. cl_a_ss p_i_ct_u_r_e_
2. f_a_m_i_l_y_
3. gr_a_d_u_a_t_i_o_n
4. b_a_b_y_
5. ph_o_t_o_ _a_lb_u_m
6. w_e_dd_i_ng

2 **Look at the pictures. Write the words from Exercise 1.**

1. Our children's ___photo album___

2. Jim and Justin at their high school
_____ – 6/5/99

3. Our _____
– 11/89

4. Jim and Deb's _____
day – 5/9/05

5. Jim and Justin's _____
_____ – June '87

6. Jim and Deb's _____
boy, Carl! – 12/11/09

Check your answers. See page 137.

3 Look at the pictures in Exercise 2. Circle the correct answers.

1. Jim and Justin became friends ____.
   a. in school _(circled)_
   b. in the hospital
   c. at work

2. They graduated from high school on ____.
   a. May 5, 1999
   b. May 6, 1999
   c. June 5, 1999 _(circled)_

3. Jim and Deb got married in ____.
   a. 1995
   b. 2005 _(circled)_
   c. 2007

4. Jim and Deb had a baby on ____.
   a. December 7, 2001
   b. November 12, 2009
   c. December 11, 2009 _(circled)_

5. Jim has ____.
   a. no brothers or sisters
   b. one sister _(circled)_
   c. one sister and one brother

4 Listen. Circle T (True) or F (False).

TRACK 21

Conversation A

1. Hee and Sue are looking at wedding pictures.   (T)   F
2. Hee got married in 1991.   T   (F)
3. Sue got married in 1993.   (T)   F

Conversation B

4. Hee and her husband got married in Los Angeles.   T   (F)
5. Hee moved to Los Angeles in 1996.   T   (F)
6. Hee's son was born in Los Angeles.   (T)   F

Conversation C

7. Hana started high school last year.   (T)   F
8. Min graduated from high school in 2012.   (T)   F
9. Min started college in 2011.   T   (F)

LESSON B When did you move here?

Study the chart on page 128.

1 Write the verbs in the past tense.

1. move   _moved_   6. start   _____
2. have   _____   7. get   _____
3. begin   _____   8. leave   _____
4. study   _____   9. meet   _____
5. find   _____   10. graduate _____

2 Complete the chart. Use the past tense forms from Exercise 1.

Regular verbs (-ed verbs)	Irregular verbs (not -ed verbs)
moved	had

3 Listen and answer the questions. Use the words in parentheses.

TRACK 22

1. When did you move here?

   (in 2000) _I moved here in 2000._

2. When did Ken start college?

   (in September) _____

3. When did you and your husband meet?

   (in 1988) _____

4. When did you get married?

   (in 1990) _____

5. When did your children begin taking English classes?

   (last year) _____

6. When did Norma leave for vacation?

   (on Saturday) _____

Check your answers. See page 137.

4 **Read Elsa's time line. Write the questions or answers. Then listen.**

TRACK 23

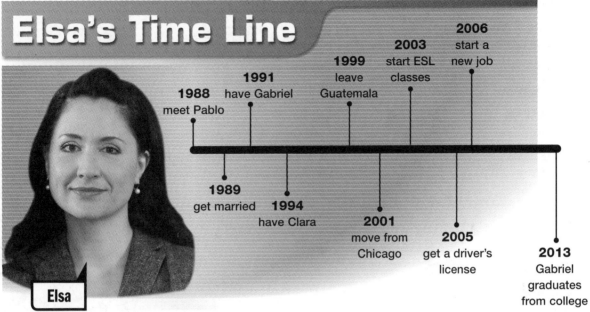

Elsa's Time Line

1988 meet Pablo

1991 have Gabriel

1999 leave Guatemala

2003 start ESL classes

2006 start a new job

1989 get married

1994 have Clara

2001 move from Chicago

2005 get a driver's license

2013 Gabriel graduates from college

Elsa

1. **A** *When did Elsa meet Pablo?*

   B Elsa met Pablo in 1988.

2. **A** _____

   B They got married in 1989.

3. **A** When did they have Gabriel?

   B _____

4. **A** _____

   B They had Clara in 1994.

5. **A** When did they leave Guatemala?

   B _____

6. **A** When did they move from Chicago to Detroit?

   B _____

7. **A** _____

   B Elsa started taking ESL classes in 2003.

8. **A** When did Elsa get her driver's license?

   B _____

Check your answers. See page 137.

LESSON C He graduated two years ago.

1 Complete the chart for events in the past.

the afternoon	half past four	a month	noon	two years
April 11th, 1990	July	the morning	Saturday	Wednesday
December	March 23rd	night	6:15	a week
four days	May 9th	1999	six months	

ago	in	on	at
	the afternoon		

2 Circle the answers.

1. Jeff and Marlena got married **ago** / (**last**) Saturday.

2. Their wedding was **in** / **on** February 1st.

3. The wedding was **at** / **this** noon.

4. They started planning the wedding eight months **ago** / **last**.

5. Marlena found her dress **in** / **on** December.

6. They left for their honeymoon **on** / **this** morning.

7. They need to return **before** / **on** Jeff's new job begins.

8. His new job begins **in** / **on** Monday, February 10th.

9. He quit his old job just **before** / **last** they got married.

10. Marlena started her job three months **after** / **ago**.

Check your answers. See page 137.

3 Read Walter's calendar. Today is May 23rd. Complete the sentences. Use *in*, *on*, *at*, *ago*, *last*, *before*, or *after*.

May

Sunday	Monday	Tuesday	Wednesday	Thursday	Friday	Saturday
~~10~~ shop for my sister's graduation present	~~11~~ begin new job - 8:00 a.m.	~~12~~ fix my car after work	~~13~~ study for citizenship exam	~~14~~ take citizenship exam – 1:15	~~15~~ basketball game – 7:30 p.m.	~~16~~ Carina's graduation – 2:00 / dinner with family – 6:30
~~17~~	~~18~~	~~19~~ take driving test for license – 8:00 a.m.	~~20~~ doctor's appointment – 4:30	~~21~~ take books back to library	~~22~~ lunch with Carina and her boyfriend	23 lunch with Mario – noon

1. Walter had dinner with his sister Carina and her boyfriend ____last____ night.

2. He took his citizenship exam _____ Thursday, May 14th.

3. The test started _____ 1:15.

4. Walter fixed his car two days _____ he took the citizenship exam.

5. He fixed the car _____ the evening.

6. Carina's graduation was a week _____.

7. The family had dinner together _____ Carina's graduation.

8. Walter began his new job _____ week.

4 Answer the questions. Use the words in parentheses and the calendar in Exercise 3.

1. When did Walter take his driving test?

   (ago) *He took his driving test four days ago.* _____

2. When did Walter shop for his sister's graduation present?

   (last week) _____

3. When did Walter play basketball?

   (Friday, May 15th) _____

4. When did Walter have a doctor's appointment?

   (4:30) _____

5. When did Walter take his books back to the library?

   (ago) _____

LESSON D Reading

1 Read and write the correct past tense. Then listen.

TRACK 24

P.C.

Alma _immigrated_ to the United States ten years ago. In Chile, Alma
      1. immigrate
_____ with computers. Alma _____ English classes after she
   2. work   3. start
came to the United States. Alma _____ English for three years. Then,
                                      4. study
Alma _____ computer classes. Alma _____ a wonderful man
     5. begin   6. meet
named Elmer in her computer class. Alma and Elmer _____ in love.
                                             7. fall
After three months, they _____ engaged. They _____ married
                           8. get   9. get
three years ago. After they got married, they _____ good jobs in a small
                                      10. find
computer company. One year later, they got promoted. After two years, they

_____ a small computer business called PC Home Repairs. Last month,
  11. start
Alma and Elmer _____ a baby girl. They _____ to name their
                12. have   13. decide
baby Patricia Catherina. They call her P.C. for short!

2 Answer the questions. Use the information from Exercise 1.

1. When did Alma immigrate to the U.S.?

   She immigrated ten years ago.

2. When did Alma start English classes?

   _____

3. How long did Alma study English?

   _____

4. When did Alma and Elmer get married?

   _____

5. When did Alma and Elmer find jobs?

   _____

Check your answers. See page 137.

3 Number the pictures of Alma's life in the correct order. Use the information from Exercise 1.

PC Home Repairs
NOW OPEN
OPEN

a. ____

b. ____

c. _1_

d. ____

e. ____

f. ____

4 Complete the sentences. Use the information from Exercise 1.

fell in love	got promoted	retire
got engaged	had a baby	started a business
got married	immigrated	

1. Ten years ago, Alma ____*immigrated*____ to the U.S.

2. Alma and Elmer met in their computer class. Then they _____.

3. Three years ago, Alma and Elmer _____.

4. Before they got married, Alma and Elmer _____.

5. One year after they got jobs, Alma and Elmer _____.

6. Two years after they got jobs, Alma and Elmer quit and _____.

7. Last month, Alma and Elmer _____. Her name is Patricia Catherina.

8. When Alma and Elmer are 65, they will probably _____.

Check your answers. See page 137.

1 Complete the paragraph. Use the simple past.

After	~~have~~	~~in~~	~~learn~~	~~open~~	take
find	~~In~~	last	~~on~~	~~start~~	~~work~~

A Dream Comes True

Hi-sun Shen immigrated from China to the U.S. _____on_____ January

5, 2005. She __had__ a lot of plans. She __started__ English

1.   2.

classes __in__ February 2005. She __took__ English classes

  4.   5.

for two years. She also __worked__ as a server in a Chinese restaurant.

        6.

__In__ September 2006, she began vocational school. She

7.

__learned__ to be a chef in a Chinese restaurant. __After__ two years,

8.   9.

she graduated from that program. Then, she __found__ a job as a chef

                                             10.

in a Chinese restaurant. That was in September 2008. She worked there

for six years. But Hi-sun had a dream. Finally, __last__ week, Hi-sun

                                              11.

__open__ her own restaurant. She calls her restaurant Hi-sun's Dream.

12.

2 Complete the time line for Hi-sun.

a. began vocational school	d. started English classes
~~b.~~ came to the U.S.	e. worked as a chef
c. graduated from vocational school	f. worked as a server

Hi-sun's time line

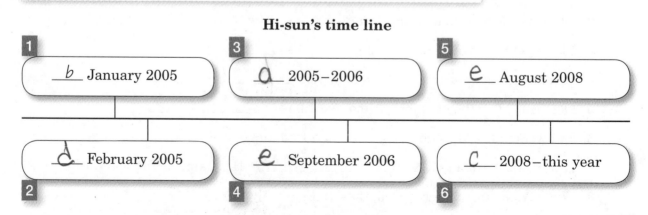

1 __b__ January 2005   **3** __d__ 2005–2006   **5** __e__ August 2008

2 __d__ February 2005   **4** __e__ September 2006   **6** __c__ 2008–this year

Check your answers. See page 138.

3 Answer the questions. Use the information from Exercises 1 and 2. Write your answers in two different ways.

1. When did Hi-sun leave China?

   On January 5, 2005, she left China.

   She left China on January 5, 2005.

2. When did she begin English classes?

   _____

   _____

3. How long did she take English classes?

   _____

   _____

4. When did she begin vocational school?

   _____

   _____

5. In what year did she graduate from vocational school?

   _____

   _____

6. When did she find a job as a chef?

   _____

   _____

7. When did she open her own restaurant?

   _____

   _____

James Johnson
Vocational School

Check your answers. See page 138.

1 **Read the questions. Look at the school application. Fill in the correct answers.**

LCC

LAGUNA COMMUNITY COLLEGE

First name ___Lin-tao___   Middle initial ___B___   Last name ___Ho___

Birthdate (Mo/Day/Yr) ___9/23/91___   Male ___X___   Female _____

Street address or P.O. box ___616 Capstone Street___

City ___Laguna___   State ___Washington___   Zip code ___98103___

E-mail address ___compwiz@cup.org___   Telephone ___206-555-1151___

Semester ___Fall 2013___

Course of study ___Computer Technology___

Educational goal ___2-year certificate___

Entry level ___First-time student in college___

High school education ___GED completed 6/12/12___

Is your primary language English?   Yes   (No)

If you circled "No": Primary language ___Mandarin___

What level is your English?

Beginner   Low-intermediate   Intermediate   High-intermediate   (Advanced)

Date of application: ___5/23/13___

1. When was Lin-tao born?
   Ⓐ 9/3/90
   ● 9/23/91
   Ⓒ 6/12/12
   Ⓓ 5/23/13

2. What does Lin-tao want to study?
   Ⓐ computer technology
   Ⓑ Mandarin
   Ⓒ English
   Ⓓ GED

3. When did Lin-tao get his GED?
   Ⓐ on June 6, 2012
   Ⓑ on June 12, 2012
   Ⓒ on December 6, 2012
   Ⓓ on May 23, 2013

4. How long is this course of study?
   Ⓐ two years
   Ⓑ two semesters
   Ⓒ two classes
   Ⓓ two weeks

5. What semester is this application for?
   Ⓐ spring
   Ⓑ summer
   Ⓒ fall
   Ⓓ winter

6. What level is Lin-tao's English?
   Ⓐ beginner
   Ⓑ intermediate
   Ⓒ high-intermediate
   Ⓓ advanced

Check your answers. See page 138.

2 **Look at the chart. Complete the conversations. Use *someone*, *anyone*, *everyone*, or *no one*.**

	Oscar	Lisa	Rob	Hong
1. Are you married?				
2. Are you single?	✓	✓	✓	✓
3. Do you have children?				
4. Do you have a brother?	✓			
5. Do you have a sister?			✓	
6. Do you have a middle name?	✓	✓	✓	✓

1. *A* Is _____*anyone*_____ married?

   B No, _____*no one*_____ is married.

2. *A* Is _____*anyone*_____ single?

   B Yes, _____*everyone*_____ is single.

3. *A* Does _____*anyone*_____ have children?

   B No, _____*no one*_____ has children.

4. *A* Does _____*anyone*_____ have a brother?

   B Yes, _____*someone*_____ has a brother.

5. *A* Does _____*anyone*_____ have a sister?

   B Yes, _____*someone*_____ has a sister.

6. *A* Does _____*anyone*_____ have a middle name?

   B Yes, _____*everyone*_____ has a middle name.

Check your answers. See page 138.

Shopping

LESSON A Listening

1 Complete the words.

1. s t __o__ v __e__
2. s ___ l ___ s p ___ r s ___ n
3. s ___ f ___
4. p ___ ___ n ___

5. c ___ s t ___ m ___ r
6. ___ p p l ___ ___ n c ___ ___
7. f ___ r n ___ t ___ r ___
8. p r ___ c ___ t ___ g

2 Look at the pictures. Write the words from Exercise 1.

1. _____ sofa _____

2. _____

3. _____

4. _____

5. _____

6. _____

7. _____

8. _____

Check your answers. See page 138.

3 Listen and complete the conversation.

TRACK 25

A Wow. They have a lot of furniture here!

B Yes. This is the biggest _____furniture_____ store in the mall.

1.

A We need help! Oh, here's someone. Are you a _____?

2.

C No, sorry. I'm a _____.

3.

D Hey, folks. I can help you. I'm Dave. I work here.

B We need some furniture. And some appliances, too.

D Well, we have furniture and _____.

4.

A We need a _____. How much is that one?

5.

D That green sofa? Let's take a look. The _____ says $999.

6.

A My goodness! How much is that sofa?

D The smaller sofa? It's actually more expensive. It's $1,059.

B Wow! We also need a _____.

7.

D Fine. We have nice pianos. This one here is only $2,000.

A What about your appliances? We need a _____.

8.

D OK. This is our best one. It's only $1,500.

A Rob, let's go. Maybe this is the biggest furniture store, but it isn't the cheapest!

Check your answers. See page 138.

LESSON B The brown sofa is bigger.

Study the chart on page 131.

1 Complete the conversations.

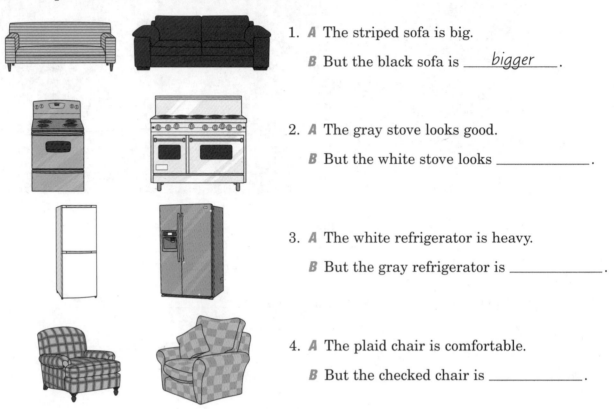

1. **A** The striped sofa is big.

   B But the black sofa is ____bigger____.

2. **A** The gray stove looks good.

   B But the white stove looks _____.

3. **A** The white refrigerator is heavy.

   B But the gray refrigerator is _____.

4. **A** The plaid chair is comfortable.

   B But the checked chair is _____.

2 Complete the conversation. Use comparatives.

A Which chair is ___more comfortable___, the blue chair or the red chair?

1. comfortable

B I don't know, but the blue chair is _____.

2. pretty

I like the pattern and the color.

A I do, too. Is it _____?

3. expensive

B Don't worry about the price. This is a thrift shop! Everything is

_____ than in a department store.

4. cheap

A Right! Well, the red chair is _____ than the blue chair.

5. big

It's _____, too.

6. heavy

B I want the blue chair.

A OK. Let's ask about the price.

Check your answers. See page 138.

3 Look at the ad and answer the questions. Then listen.

TRACK 26

MOVING SOON!
BUY MY FURNITURE!
55 LINCOLN AVE.

TABLES!
- A kitchen table for 4 people
- A dining room table for 8 people

SOFAS!
- A green sofa for 6 people
- A white sofa for 3 people

APPLIANCES!
- Stove: $200
- Refrigerator: $250

DESKS!
- A blue desk – 2005
- A silver desk – 2011

CHAIRS!
- Red chairs for children
- White chairs for the kitchen

LAMPS!
- A green floor lamp
- A black table lamp

1. **A** Which table is bigger?

   B *The dining room table is bigger.* _____

2. **A** Which chairs are smaller?

   B _____

3. **A** Which appliance is more expensive?

   B _____

4. **A** Which desk is older?

   B _____

5. **A** Which sofa is longer?

   B _____

6. **A** Which lamp is shorter?

   B _____

Check your answers. See page 138.

LESSON C The yellow chair is the cheapest.

Study the chart on page 131.

1 Complete the chart. Write the comparative and superlative forms of the adjectives.

	Adjective	Comparative	Superlative
1.	expensive	*more expensive*	*the most expensive*
2.	cheap		
3.	friendly		
4.	good		
5.	new		
6.	heavy		
7.	low		
8.	beautiful		
9.	pretty		
10.	crowded		
11.	comfortable		
12.	nice		

2 Complete the sentences. Use superlatives.

1. Furniture First has _____*the lowest*_____ prices of all the furniture stores.
   (low)

2. Robinson's Furniture has _____ chairs.
   (comfortable)

3. Jay Mart's clothes are _____ clothes in the mall.
   (good)

4. Curto's has _____ appliances in town.
   (expensive)

5. Which store has _____ salespeople?
   (nice)

6. Bella's clothes are _____ in the mall.
   (pretty)

7. The furniture at Secondhand Row is _____ in town.
   (cheap)

8. Appliance World is _____ of all the appliance stores.
   (crowded)

9. The SuperPlus TVs are _____ TVs in the store.
   (heavy)

Check your answers. See page 138.

3 Complete the chart.

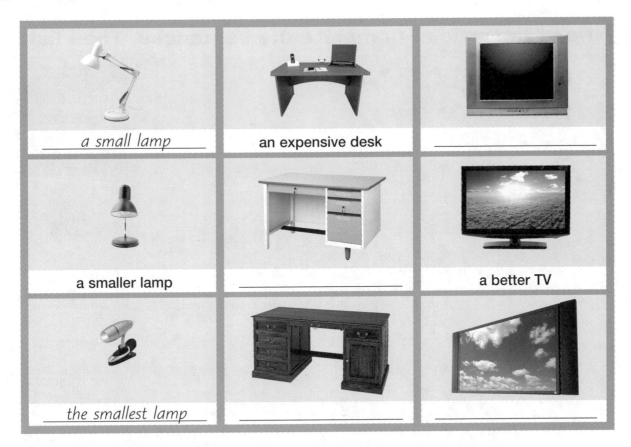

a small lamp	an expensive desk	_____
a smaller lamp	_____	a better TV
the smallest lamp	_____	_____

4 Answer the questions.

Clothing for Today's Woman

A. jeans skirt $40   B. tennis skirt $55   C. evening skirt $150

1. Which skirt is the most expensive?

   The evening skirt is the most expensive.

2. Which skirt is the longest?

   _____

3. Which skirt is the cheapest?

   _____

4. Which skirt is the shortest?

   _____

LESSON D Reading

1 Read the article. Complete the sentences. Then listen.

Centerville's Newest Old Store
by Joe Jordan

Antique Alley is the _____newest_____ store in Centerville.
1. new

Antique Alley opened on May 1st, and now it's having a _____ sale. Everything is
2. big

50% to 75% off. Those are the _____ prices for old furniture in Centerville.
3. good

I visited Antique Alley yesterday. The furniture is _____ . For me, the
4. beautiful

_____ thing in the store was a large mirror. I didn't buy it because it was also the
5. nice

_____ thing in the store. It was $1,300! Of course, it was also the _____
6. expensive   7. old

thing in the store. It was 300 years old. But there were things that were _____
8. cheap

than the mirror. The _____ thing was a _____ lamp for only $12.95.
9. cheap   10. small

Visit Antique Alley this weekend. You'll be surprised at what you find.

2 Answer the questions.

1. What is the name of the store?

   The name of the store is Antique Alley.

2. When did it open?

   _____

3. What was the most expensive thing in the store?

   _____

4. How much was it?

   _____

5. What was the cheapest thing in the store?

   _____

6. How much was it?

   _____

Check your answers. See page 138.

3 Complete the puzzle.

aquarium   computer desk   entertainment center   mirror   sofa bed

bookcase   end table   furniture   recliner

Down

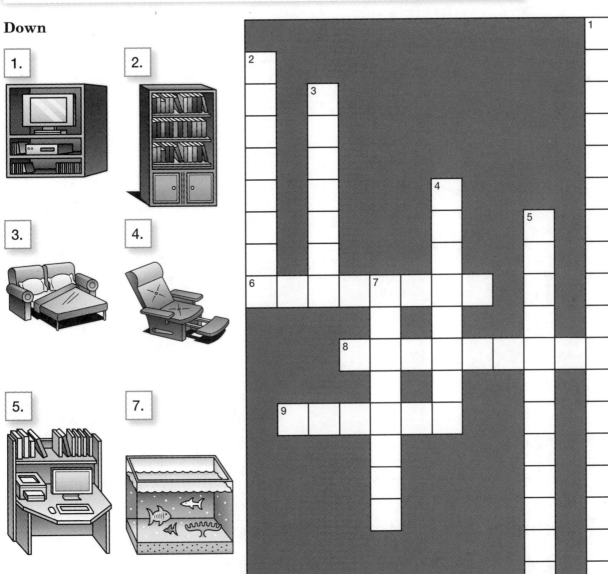

1.

2.

3.

4.

5.

7.

Across

6.

8.

9.

Check your answers. See page 139.

LESSON E Writing

1 Read the note. Answer the questions.

Dear Miguel,

This is a special gift because it is your 40th birthday. This is an airline ticket to Mexico. You can visit your brother there. I know you miss him. Happy birthday!

Your loving wife,
Amelia

✈ Central Airlines

Departing from:
New York

Going to:
Mexico City

Leave on:
August 10

1. Who is the gift for?
   The gift is for Miguel.

2. Who is the gift from?
   _____

3. What did she give him?
   _____

4. Why did he receive the gift?
   _____

5. Where will he go?
   _____

6. What day will he leave?
   _____

2 Combine the sentences. Use *because*.

1. I bought the red sofa. It was the most comfortable.
   I bought the red sofa because it was the most comfortable.

2. Sandra gave her sister a pair of earrings. It was her birthday.
   _____

3. Mr. and Mrs. Chung shop at the Clothes Corner. It's the nicest store.
   _____

4. Roberto bought the brown recliner. It was on sale.
   _____

5. I bought an entertainment center. It was 50 percent off.
   _____

Check your answers. See page 139.

3 Read the chart. Complete the sentences. Use the comparative or superlative.

CENTERVILLE DEPARTMENT STORES				
	Opened	Size	Prices	Comments
Best Discounts	1983	40,000 square feet	very low	nice salespeople
Smart Deparment Store	2013	60,000 square feet	very high	beautiful, not crowded
Super Discounts	1970	20,000 square feet	medium	crowded

Yesterday, I needed to buy a lot of things, so I went shopping at Best Discounts.

Smart Department Store is _____*bigger*_____ than Best Discounts, but the salespeople
                                    1. big

are _____ at Best Discounts. Also, the prices at Best Discounts are
          2. nice

_____ than at Smart Department Store. Smart Department Store is
     3. good

_____ than Best Discounts, and it's also _____ than Best
     4. new   5. beautiful

Discounts, but the prices are _____.
                                  6. high

I never go to Super Discounts. It's the _____ department store in town.
                                              7. old

It's the _____, and it's always the _____.
            8. small   9. crowded

4 Complete the sentences. Use the chart in Exercise 3. Use the superlative.

1. (small)   _____*Super Discounts*_____ is _____*the smallest*_____.

2. (old)   _____ is _____.

3. (big)   _____ is _____.

4. (expensive) _____ is _____.

5. (cheap)   _____ is _____.

6. (crowded)   _____ is _____.

LESSON F Another view

1 **Read the questions. Look at the ads. Fill in the correct answers.**

Closing Sale. 25-50% off
everything in the store.
Come and look!
Used furniture in good condition!
Hours: 9 a.m. to midnight,
7 days a week.
Deliveries on weekends only.

BIG BILL'S
BEST
FURNITURE

FATHER'S DAY
SALE!

All recliners and chairs on sale.
New and used! Only the best.
30-40% discounts.
FREE DELIVERY.

Hours:
8:00 a.m. – 6:00 p.m.
Mon. – Sat.

MODERN FURNITURE

Everything on sale! 50–80% off. China Cabinets, Bookcases, Beds,
Sofa Beds, Coffee Tables, Entertainment Centers, Kitchen Appliances.
We have it all. It's all new!

HOURS: 11:00 – 9:00 MONDAY THROUGH FRIDAY AND 12:00 – 9:00 ON SATURDAY.
BRING A VAN AND TAKE IT HOME. EXTRA FOR DELIVERY.

---

1. Which store has only used furniture?
   Ⓐ Big Bill's
   Ⓑ Modern Furniture
   ● Nick's Nearly New
   Ⓓ all of the above

2. Which store makes deliveries?
   Ⓐ Big Bill's
   Ⓑ Modern Furniture
   Ⓒ Nick's Nearly New
   Ⓓ all of the above

3. Which store has new and used furniture?
   Ⓐ Big Bill's
   Ⓑ Modern Furniture
   Ⓒ Nick's Nearly New
   Ⓓ all of the above

4. Which store has a Father's Day Sale?
   Ⓐ Big Bill's
   Ⓑ Modern Furniture
   Ⓒ Nick's Nearly New
   Ⓓ all of the above

5. Which store is open on Sunday?
   Ⓐ Big Bill's
   Ⓑ Modern Furniture
   Ⓒ Nick's Nearly New
   Ⓓ all of the above

6. At which store do you pay extra for delivery?
   Ⓐ Big Bill's
   Ⓑ Modern Furniture
   Ⓒ Nick's Nearly New
   Ⓓ all of the above

Check your answers. See page 139.

2 **Look at the ad. Complete the sentences. Use *one*, *some*, *the other*, and *the others*.**

ONE-DAY SALE!

Clothes and Accessories

Purses

$50

$15

$15 $50

Necklaces

$30

$25

Shirts

$20 $20 $20

$18 $18 $18

Furniture

Tables

$75 $100

Armchairs

$150 $25

1. There are two necklaces. _____One_____ is long, and __the other__ is short.

2. The necklaces are cheap. _____ is $30, and _____ is $25.

3. There are four purses. _____ are big, and _____ are small.

4. The purses are nice. _____ are $15, and _____ are $50.

5. There are six shirts. _____ are white, and _____ are striped.

6. The shirts are different prices. _____ are $20, and _____ are $18.

7. There are two chairs. _____ is expensive, and _____ is cheap.

8. I like the chairs. _____ is $150, and _____ is only $25.

9. There are two tables. _____ is round, and _____ is square.

10. The tables are nice. _____ is $75, and _____ is $100.

Check your answers. See page 139.

LESSON A Listening

1 **Unscramble the letters. Write the words.**

1. bla _____lab_____
2. derlyor _____
3. oc-rkerwos _____
4. kerwal _____

5. inensl _____
6. tentiap _____
7. liessupp _____
8. hailwhreec _____

2 **Look at the picture. Write the words from Exercise 1.**

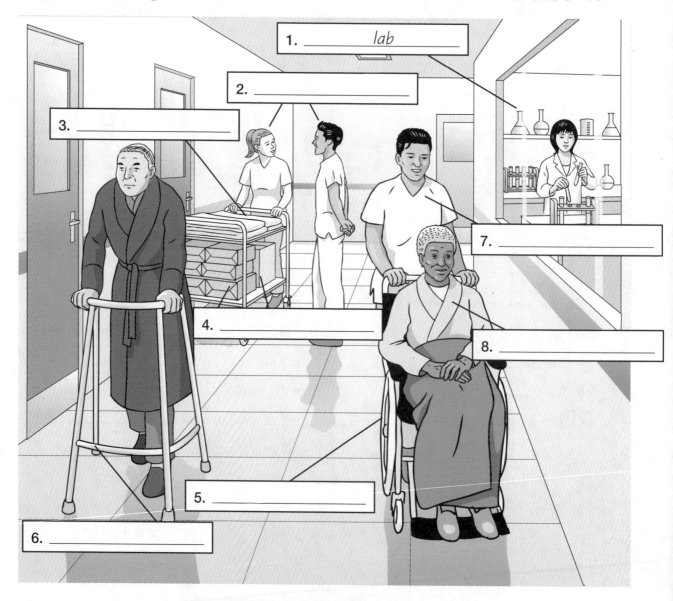

1. _____lab_____
2. _____
3. _____
4. _____
5. _____
6. _____
7. _____
8. _____

Check your answers. See page 139.

3 Complete the sentences.

| co-workers | linens | orderly | patient | walker | wheelchair |

1. The ____patient____ came to the hospital with a broken leg.

2. Suzanne and her two _____ worked the night shift together.

3. Suzanne put clean _____ on the bed.

4. Because he broke his leg, Sam had to ride in a _____.

5. The _____ took the X-rays to the lab.

6. Anne is very old. She needs to use a _____ when she walks.

4 Listen. Circle T (True) or F (False).

TRACK 28

Conversation A

1. Otto has a new job.	T	F
2. Otto delivered a walker to a patient yesterday.	T	F
3. Otto cleans rooms.	T	F

Conversation B

4. Otto started his job a few months ago.	T	F
5. Otto needs to work full-time now.	T	F
6. Otto wants to be a medical assistant.	T	F

Conversation C

7. Otto is in an office at Valley Hospital.	T	F
8. Otto can go to school part-time and work part-time.	T	F
9. Otto can't take classes at night.	T	F

5 Make the false statements in Exercise 4 true. Write.

_____

_____

_____

_____

LESSON B Where did you go last night?

Study the chart on page 128.

1 Match the questions with the answers.

1. Where did you go last night? __c__
2. What did you take to the party? __e__
3. What did Cristal do after breakfast? __b__
4. Where did your parents meet? __g__
5. What did they do after they came to the U.S.? __a__
6. What did Jon pick up at your house? __d__
7. Where did you and Andy go this morning? __f__

a. They worked in restaurants.
b. She cleaned the house.
c. I went to the movies.
d. He picked up a uniform.
e. I took a cake to the party.
f. We went to the beach.
g. They met at school.

2 Read the answers. Write *What* or *Where*.

1. **A** ___What___ did you do last night?

   B I worked the night shift.

2. **A** _Where_ did you go after work?

   B I went out for breakfast.

3. **A** _Where_ did Max do after breakfast?

   B He took the bus to school.

4. **A** _What_ did Sheila do at work this morning?

   B She made the beds with new linens.

5. **A** _what_ did you and your family eat dinner last night?

   B We ate dinner at Tony's Pizzeria.

6. **A** _what_ did Sheila and Max do last weekend?

   B They went to the park for a picnic.

7. **A** _Where_ did you do after the concert?

   B We went for coffee.

8. **A** _what_ did Max go last Sunday?

   B He went to the baseball game.

Check your answers. See page 139.

3 **Read and complete the questions and answers.**
Use *What* or *Where* and the simple past. Then listen.

TRACK 29

Mai
- meet new patients in reception area–9:00
- take the patient in Room 304 to the lab–9:30
- make the bed in Room 304
- take patients from lab to their rooms–10:00
- help nurses on the fourth floor–10:45
- lunch in the cafeteria–12:30

Jorge
- meet new patients in reception area–9:00
- pick up X-rays from lab–9:30
- deliver X-rays to doctors
- help patient in Room 310–10:00
- prepare rooms on the second floor –11:30
- lunch in the cafeteria–12:30

---

1. A _____What_____ did Mai and Jorge do at 9:00?
   B They meet a new patients.

2. A __Where__ did Mai take her patient at 9:30?
   B She took the patient to the lab.

3. A __What.__ did Jorge do at 9:30?
   B He pick up X-rays from lab.

4. A __what__ did Mai and Jorge do after 9:30?
   B Mai __made the bed__, and Jorge __delivered X rays.__

5. A __Where__ did Jorge go at 10:00?
   B He help the patient

6. A __what__ did Jorge do in Room 310?
   B He help the patient

7. A __what__ did Mai do at 10:00?
   B She took to the nurses on room 4.

8. A __where__ did Mai go after that?
   B She went to the family room

9. A __what__ did Jorge do at 11:30?
   B He prapared rooms on the second Floor.

Check your answers. See page 139.

LESSON C I work on Saturdays and Sundays.

1 Complete the sentences. Use *and*, *or*, or *but*.

1. Mateo has two jobs. He works in a restaurant ____*and*____ in an office.

2. We can have lunch at Sub's ____or____ at Carl's.

3. Gu-jan talked to his mother about his job plans, ____but____ he didn't talk to his father.

4. After work, Lourdes had cake ____and____ ice cream.

5. Mandy and Paco went to New York, ____but____ they didn't see the Statue of Liberty.

6. Ivan works the day shift ____or____ the night shift. He never works both shifts.

7. Sally works at the hospital during the week ____and____ at Pizza Town on the weekend.

8. At work, Ang answers the phones ____and____ takes messages.

2 Combine the sentences. Use *and*, *or*, or *but*.

1. Sometimes Jun eats lunch at noon. Sometimes Jun eats lunch at 1:00.

   Jun eats lunch at noon or at 1:00.

2. Javier helps the nurses. He also helps the doctors.

   Javier helps the nurses, and he also helps the doctor.

3. Tien picks up the supplies at the warehouse. She doesn't deliver the supplies.

   Tien picks up the supplies at the warehouse, but she didn't deliver the supplies.

4. Rieko met her new co-workers this morning. She didn't meet any patients.

   Rieko met her new co-workers this morning, but didn't meet any patients.

5. At the restaurant, Mustafa made the soup. He also made the salad.

   At the restaurant, Mustafa made the soup and he also made the salad.

6. Sometimes Anatoly drinks coffee. Sometimes he drinks tea.

   Sometimes Anatoly drinks coffe and he drink tea.

Check your answers. See page 139.

3 Read the chart. Write sentences. Use *and* or *but* and the simple past.

Office Assistant Duties – Friday 11/29		
Rachel	**Dora**	**Adam**
Prepare the meeting room	Make the coffee	Check the office e-mail
Pick up supplies	Go to the meeting	Go to the meeting
Deliver the mail	Answer calls	Take notes
	Take messages	Make copies

1. Dora / go to the meeting / take notes

   Dora went to the meeting, but she didn't take notes.

2. Adam / check the office e-mail / go to the meeting

   Adam check the office e-mail, and went to the meeting

3. Rachel / prepare the meeting room / make the coffee

   Rachel prepare the meeting room and make the coffe

4. Dora and Adam / go to the meeting / prepare the meeting room

   Dora an Ada went to the meeting, but didn't the prepare the meeting room.

5. Adam / take notes / make copies

   Adan took notes and made copies.

6. Rachel / pick up supplies / deliver the mail

   Rachel picked up supplies, and delivered the mail.

4 Complete the sentences with *and, or,* or *but*.

Please eat lunch at your desk and answer calls on these days:					
	Monday	Tuesday	Wednesday	Thursday	Friday
This week	Rachel	Dora	Adam	Dora	Adam
Next week	Adam	Dora	Rachel	Dora	Adam

1. Dora eats lunch at her desk on Tuesday ___and___ Thursday.

2. On Monday, Rachel ___or___ Adam answer calls. *(enser)*

3. This week, Adam eats lunch at his desk on Wednesday ___and___ Friday.

4. Dora and Adam eat lunch at their desks twice a week, ___but___

   Rachel doesn't. She eats lunch at her desk only once a week.

Check your answers. See pages 139–140.

LESSON D Reading

1 Read and circle the correct answers. Then listen.

TRACK 30

WESTPORT COMMUNITY **COLLEGE** _____ **WCC**

May 25, 2013

To Whom It May Concern:

    I am happy to write this letter of recommendation for Federico Robles. Federico is a student in the Medical Assistant Certificate Program here at WCC. He will graduate in June.

    Federico is an excellent student and a hard worker. He can manage a medical office, schedule appointments, and take care of patient records. He can assist doctors with many duties.

    I recommend Federico very highly. He will be an excellent medical assistant. Please contact me for more information.

Sincerely,

Carrie McIntosh

Carrie McIntosh, Instructor

1. Carrie McIntosh is Federico's ____.
   a. boss
   b. medical assistant
   c. instructor *(circled)*

2. This letter of recommendation is about ____.
   a. Carrie McIntosh
   b. Federico
   c. Federico's new boss

3. Federico can ____.
   a. manage a medical office
   b. schedule appointments
   c. both a and b

4. Federico ____.
   a. is looking for a job
   b. is going to start school
   c. has a job now

5. In June, Federico is going to ____.
   a. get a new job
   b. graduate
   c. quit his job

6. In this program, Federico learned to ____.
   a. assist doctors
   b. take care of patients
   c. teach medical assistants

2 Answer the questions.

1. Who wrote the letter? *Carrie McIntosh wrote the letter.*

2. When did she write the letter? _____

3. Where does she teach? _____

4. What program does she teach in? _____

5. What job skills did Federico learn? List them. _____

_____

Check your answers. See page 140.

3 Match the jobs with the pictures.

a.

b.

c.

d.

e.

f.

g.

h.

1. auto mechanic
2. orderly
3. homemaker
4. cashier
5. construction worker
6. medical assistant
7. cook
8. teacher

4 Complete the sentences. Use the jobs from Exercise 3.

1. A _____*homemaker*_____ takes care of a family.

2. A _____construction worker_____ operates large machines.

3. An _____ helps the nurses.

4. A _____ assists the doctor.

5. An _____ repairs cars.

6. A _____ teaches students.

7. A _____ handles money.

8. A _____ prepares food.

Check your answers. See page 140.

LESSON E Writing

1 **Read Michael's employment history. Complete the sentences. Use the correct form of the verb.**

Employment History: Michael Bitter

Michael Bitter is a medical assistant. He _____ at Valley Medical Clinic. He started
                                              1. work

in 2008. He _____ appointments for patients. He _____ the phones and
                 2. make   3. answer

_____ messages. He _____ the patients and _____ the doctors.
   4. take   5. prepare   6. assist

From 1994 to 2006, Michael _____ at Freshie's Pizza. He had two jobs there. From 2002
                                 7. work

to 2006, he _____ a cashier. He _____ money and _____ the credit card
               8. be   9. handle   10. operate

machine. From 1994 to 2002, he _____ a busperson.
                                      11. be

Michael _____ to Westport Community College from 2006 to 2008. He _____
            12. go   13. be

a full-time student in the Medical Assistant Certificate Program. He _____ in June 2008.
                                                                          14. graduate

In June 2003, he _____ his GED at Staples Adult School.
                     15. get

---

2 **Answer the questions. Use the employment history in Exercise 1.**

1. When did Michael start his job at the medical clinic?

   He started his job at the medical clinic in 2008.

2. Where did he work for 12 years?

   _____

3. What did he do from 2006 to 2008?

   _____

4. Where did he study for his GED?

   _____

5. When did he get his GED?

   _____

6. Where does he work now?

   _____

Check your answers. See page 140.

3 Rewrite the sentences. Use the simple past.

1. I prepare food, but I don't clear the tables.

   I prepared food, but I didn't clear the tables.

2. I handle money and talk to people every day.

   _____

3. I help the nurses, but I don't help the doctors.

   _____

4. I take care of my children and my house.

   _____

5. I clear tables and handle money, but I don't prepare food.

   _____

6. I operate large machines and build houses.

   _____

4 Match the pictures with the sentences in Exercise 3. Then write the words.

busperson	construction worker	homemaker
cashier	cook	orderly

a. ____

_____

b. _1_

cook

c. ____

_____

d. ____

_____

e. ____

_____

f. ____

_____

LESSON F Another view

1 Read the job ads. Write the words. Start each word with a capital letter.

auto mechanic   busperson   cashier   construction worker   medical assistant   orderly

1. _____Orderly_____ Needed.
Help patients walk, take patients for X-rays, deliver X-rays and mail, help nurses, talk to patients. No experience necessary.

2. _____ Wanted.
You will need to handle money, use a cash register, know basic math, be friendly with customers, and be on time. Restaurant experience necessary.

3. _____ Needed.
You need to have two years of experience building houses. Need a driver's license. Need to be able to work alone.

4. _____ Wanted.
Medical office needs friendly worker. Assist doctor and take care of office. Experience or Medical Assistant Certificate needed.

5. _____ Needed.
Busy car repair shop needs worker. Experience with American and foreign cars useful. Five years of experience necessary.

6. _____ Wanted.
New restaurant needs worker to clear and clean tables. No experience necessary. Need to work fast.

2 Read the sentences. Which job is best for each person? Write the jobs from Exercise 1.

1. I am friendly and like to help people.   _____orderly_____

2. I like to use tools and machines.   _____

3. I can handle money, and I like math.   _____

4. I repaired cars for seven years.   _____

5. I cleared tables in a restaurant last year.   _____

6. I like to work alone.   _____

7. I have a Medical Assistant Certificate.   _____

8. I can work fast.   _____

Check your answers. See page 140.

3 Look at the chart. Write sentences about Dani. Use *can*, *can't*, *could*, and *couldn't*.

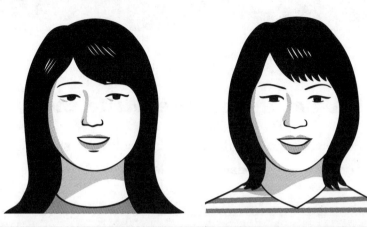

	Ten years ago	Now
cook	No	Yes
dance	Yes	No
drive	No	No
run fast	Yes	No
play the piano	Yes	Yes
read English	No	Yes
speak Spanish	No	Yes
take care of a family	No	Yes

1. Dani _____*couldn't*_____ cook ten years ago, but she _____*can*_____ cook now.

2. Dani _____ dance ten years ago, but she _____ dance now.

3. Dani _____ drive ten years ago, and she _____ drive now.

4. Dani _____ run fast ten years ago, but she _____ run fast now.

5. Dani _____ play the piano ten years ago, and she _____ play the piano now.

6. Dani _____ read English ten years ago, but she _____ read English now.

7. Dani _____ speak Spanish ten years ago, but she _____ speak Spanish now.

8. Dani _____ take care of a family ten years ago, but she _____ take care of a family now.

Check your answers. See page 140.

LESSON **A** Listening

1 **Look at the picture. Write the words.**

dishwasher	garbage	lightbulb	sink
dryer	leak	lock	washing machine

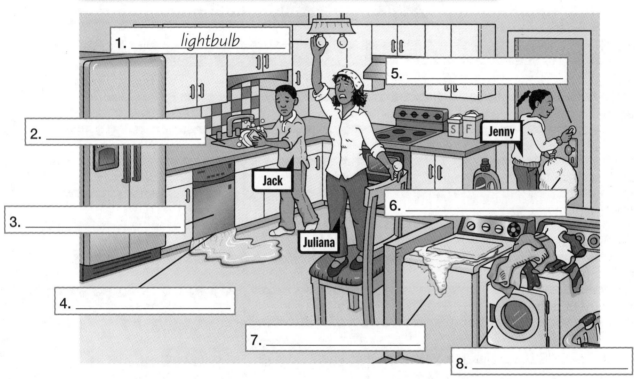

1. _____lightbulb_____
2. _____
3. _____
4. _____
5. _____
6. _____
7. _____
8. _____

Jack   Jenny   Juliana

2 **Complete the sentences. Use the words from Exercise 1.**

1. Jenny is taking out the _____garbage_____.

2. She is unlocking the door. Her hand is on the _____.

3. Juliana is changing a _____.

4. Jack is washing the dishes in the _____.

5. There is water on the floor in front of the _____.

6. The dishwasher has a _____.

7. There is soapy water coming from the _____.

8. There are clothes on top of the _____.

Check your answers. See page 140.

3 Look at the picture in Exercise 1. Answer the questions.

1. How many appliances does Juliana have in her kitchen?

   She has five appliances in her kitchen.

2. Which appliances does she have?

   _____

3. How many appliances have problems?

   _____

4. Which appliances have problems?

   _____

4 Listen. Circle the correct answers.

TRACK 31

Conversation A

1. Who is Steve calling?
   a. a neighbor
   b. the building manager
   c. a plumber

2. Steve has a problem with _____.
   a. the sink and the dishwasher
   b. the washing machine and the dishwasher
   c. the washing machine and the sink

3. The better plumber is _____.
   a. the Brown Plumbing Company
   b. the Green Company
   c. Gemelli Plumbers

Conversation B

4. Who is Linda?
   a. a neighbor
   b. a receptionist
   c. a building manager

5. Steve lives on _____.
   a. 15th Street
   b. Second Avenue
   c. Fourth Street

6. Mark can come _____.
   a. at 9:00
   b. at noon
   c. at 4:00

Conversation C

7. Who is Steve calling?
   a. a neighbor
   b. a plumber
   c. the building manager

8. When did Ms. Ling's sink overflow?
   a. last month
   b. last week
   c. this morning

9. When will Ms. Ling be back?
   a. at 9:00
   b. at 10:00
   c. at 11:00

Check your answers. See page 140.

LESSON B Can you call a plumber, please?

1 Rewrite the questions. Use the words in parentheses.

1. Can you call a plumber, please?

   (Could) *Could you call a plumber, please?*

2. Could you fix the window, please?

   (Would) _____

3. Would you fix the lock, please?

   (Will) _____

4. Could you fix the dryer, please?

   (Would) _____

5. Would you unclog the sink, please?

   (Could) _____

6. Would you fix the stove, please?

   (Can) _____

2 Circle the correct answers.

1. Could you fix the window?
   a. No, I'd be happy to.
   b. Yes, of course.

2. Would you repair the dishwasher?
   a. Sorry, I can't right now.
   b. Sorry, I'd be happy to.

3. Can you unclog the sink?
   a. No, of course.
   b. Yes, I'd be happy to.

4. Will you fix the lock now, please?
   a. No, not now. Maybe later.
   b. No, I'd be happy to.

5. Could you call an electrician now, please?
   a. Sure. Maybe later.
   b. Yes, of course.

6. Would you repair the toilet now, please?
   a. No, I can right now.
   b. Sorry, I can't right now.

Check your answers. See page 140.

3 Look at the picture. Make requests for the landlord.

1. A <u>Could you fix the window, please?</u>
   (Could / fix / window)

   B Sure, I'd be happy to.

2. A <u>Would you repair the refrigerator please?</u>
   (Would / repair / refrigerator)

   B No, not now. Maybe later.

3. A <u>Can you fix the light?</u>
   (Can / fix / light)

   B Yes, of course.

4. A <u>Will you unclog the sink?</u>
   (Will / unclog / sink)

   B Sorry, I can't right now.

5. A <u>Could you repair the lock?</u>
   (Could / repair / lock)

   B No, not now. Maybe later.

6. A <u>Would you fix the dishwasher?</u>
   (Would / fix / dishwasher)

   B Yes, of course. I'd be happy to.

4 Read the list. Listen and make requests with *Could*.

TRACK 32

1. A <u>Could you fix the light, please?</u>

   B No, maybe later.

2. A <u>Could you unclog the bathtub Please?</u>

   B Yes, of course.

3. A <u>Could you repair the dishwasher please?</u>

   B Sorry, I can't right now.

4. A <u>Could you clean the carpet, please?</u>

   B Sure. I'd be happy to.

5. A <u>Could you change the lightbulb please?</u>

   B Yes, of course.

6. A <u>Could you call the plumber please?</u>

   B No, maybe later.

1. ~~fix the light~~
2. ~~unclog the bathtub~~
3. ~~change the lightbulb~~
4. ~~repair the dishwasher~~
5. ~~clean the carpet~~
6. call a plumber

Check your answers. See pages 140–141.

LESSON C Which one do you recommend?

Study the chart on page 127.

1 Complete each question with *do* or *does*. Then write the answer.

1. Which plumber _____*do*_____ they recommend?
   (Jerry's Plumbing) *They recommend Jerry's Plumbing.*

2. Which teacher _____does_____ he recommend?
   (Joe Thompson) He recommends Joe ?

3. Which electrician _____do_____ you recommend?
   (Wired Electric) I recommend wired Electric

4. Which pharmacy _____do_____ they recommend?
   (Rite Price) They recommend Rite Price

5. Which bank _____does_____ she recommend?
   (Bank and Trust) She recommends Bank and Trust

6. Which supermarket _____does_____ he recommend?
   (SaveMore) He recommends SaveMore.

2 Answer the questions. Use the words in parentheses.

1. Which babysitter does Marian recommend?
   (her cousin) *Marian recommends her cousin.*

2. Which plumber do you suggest?
   (Drains R Us) I suggest Drains R Us.

3. Which auto mechanic does your husband like?
   (Ed Peterson) He likes Ed Peterson.

4. Which doctor does your daughter recommend?
   (Dr. White) She recommend Dr. white

5. Which supermarket do you and your family like?
   (Food City) We like Food City

6. Which ESL program does your wife recommend?
   (Rockland Adult School) She recommends Rockland Adult School

7. Which clinic do you and your husband suggest?
   (the City Clinic) We suggest the City Clinic

Check your answers. See page 141.

3 Read the ads. Circle the answers.

1. It's Saturday, and your friend's dishwasher has a leak.

   You recommend **Fix It** / **(ABC.)**

2. You want a licensed repair person to fix your dryer.

   Your friend recommends **Fix It** / **ABC**.

3. Your mother needs a repair person for her stove right now.

   You recommend **Fix It** / **ABC**.

4. You want the repair person to clean the floor after the job is finished.

   Your parents recommend **Fix It** / **ABC**.

4 Read the ads. Write the answers. Give reasons.

1. Which locksmith do you recommend?

   (All Keys / 24 hours) _I recommend All Keys because it's open 24 hours._

2. Which locksmith do they suggest?

   (Smitty's / licensed) _____

3. Which locksmith does Harry like?

   (All Keys / more experienced) _____

4. Which locksmith does Muriel suggest?

   (Smitty's / free keys) _____

5. Which locksmith do the Corwins recommend?

   (All Keys / fast service) _____

LESSON D Reading

1 Read and circle the correct answers. Then listen.

From: Rico Martinez <rmar14@cup.org>

To: Jenna and Enrique Martinez <jem45@cup.org>

Date: January 8, 2013

Subject: NEW APARTMENT

Hi Mom and Dad,

How are you? We're all fine. We moved into our new apartment one week ago. It's very nice. There are some problems, but our landlord will fix them. There are two big bedrooms – one for the children and one for us. The carpet in the children's bedroom is stained, but the landlord is going to put in a new carpet tomorrow. Also, the curtains in our bedroom are torn. Claudia is going to make new curtains for all the rooms. She bought some beautiful material on sale. Some of the windows are jammed, but they are very big. It's winter now, and we don't need to open them. The landlord will fix them before spring. It's a really nice apartment. The rooms are big and sunny. Come and visit us soon!

Love,
Rico

1. What is the landlord going to do tomorrow?
   a. fix the windows
   b. put in a new carpet
   c. repair the curtains

2. What is Claudia going to do?
   a. fix the curtains
   b. make new curtains
   c. wash the curtains

3. Rico is not upset about the jammed windows. Why?
   a. because it's cold outside
   b. because it's hot outside
   c. because the landlord will fix them tomorrow

4. What is the problem in the children's bedroom?
   a. The windows are broken.
   b. The curtains are torn.
   c. The carpet is stained.

5. Why does Rico like the windows?
   a. They are new.
   b. They are big.
   c. They are not cracked.

6. What does Rico like about the apartment?
   a. It's sunny and the rooms are big.
   b. The landlord is nice.
   c. The curtains are beautiful.

Check your answers. See page 141.

2 Look at the picture. Write the words.

~~bent~~	~~cracked~~	scratched
~~broken~~	~~dripping~~	~~stained~~
~~burned out~~	~~jammed~~	~~torn~~

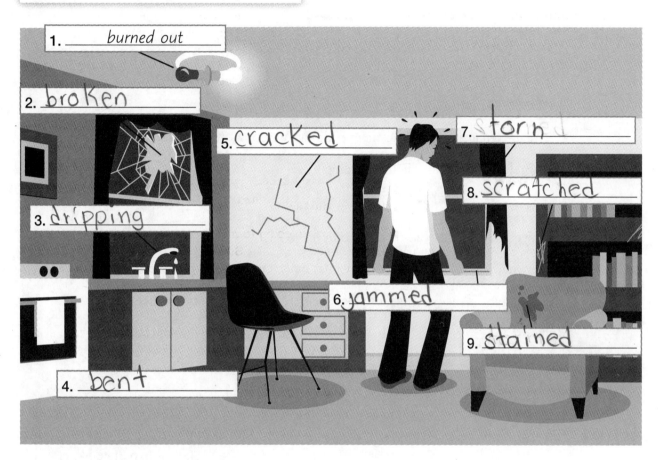

1. _burned out_
2. _broken_
3. _dripping_
4. _bent_
5. _cracked_
6. _jammed_
7. _torn_
8. _scratched_
9. _stained_

3 Complete the sentences. Use words from Exercise 2.

1. One window won't open. It's _jammed_.
2. The other window is _broken_.
3. One lightbulb is _burned out_.
4. The faucet in the kitchen is _dripping_.
5. The curtain is _torn_.
6. The wall is _cracked_.
7. One chair has a _bent_ leg.
8. The other chair is _bent_.
9. The bookcase is _scratched_.

Check your answers. See page 141.

LESSON E Writing

1 Read the letter. Write the words.

~~broken~~	~~clogged~~	~~dripping~~	scratched
~~burned out~~	~~cracked~~	~~jammed~~	~~stained~~

December 2, 2013

Dear Ms. Torrant,

We are tenants in your apartment building. We are writing this letter because we are upset about problems in the building.

There are _____broken_____ windows and many _cracked_ ceilings.
       1.   2.
You need to paint the walls because they are _stained_. We can't open
                                 3.
some windows because they are _jammed_. You need to replace many of
                             4.
the lightbulbs in the halls because they are _burned out_. Some faucets in the
                        5.
sinks are _dripping_. Also, many doors are _scratched_, and some toilets
          6.   7.
are _clogged_.
     8.

Please reply to Jim Bowen in Apartment 822. Thank you for your attention.

Sincerely,
The tenants of 616 State Street

Sharmin Patel Apt. 201   *Randy Jones* Apt. 412   *Brad Wilson* Apt. 605

2 Answer the questions. Use the information from Exercise 1.

1. How many signatures can you see? _Three signatures._
2. List all the apartment numbers in the letter. _Three apartments 201, 412, 60_
3. What is the date of this letter? _December 2, 2013._
4. Who is the letter to? _Ms. Torrant_
5. What is the closing of the letter? _Sincerely_
6. How many paragraphs are there in the body of the letter? _3 paragraphs._
7. Who should Ms. Torrant reply to? _Jim Bowen in apartment 802_

    Check your answers. See page 141.

3 **Read the list of problems. Complete the letter of complaint.**

List of Problems for:
78 Hillspoint Road Apartments

Apartment	Problem
4B	Leaking dishwasher
6A	Stained carpet
1B	~~Cracked bathtub~~
2C	Clogged toilet
3A	Broken stove

July 3, 2013

Dear Mr. Treelake,

I am a tenant in your apartment building at 78 Hillspoint Road. I am writing to you about some problems in the apartments.

Apartment 1B has a _cracked bathtub_ . The _dishwasher_ in
Apartment 4 B is _leaking_ 3. . The tenants in Apartment 2C have
a _clogged toilet_ . Could you please call a plumber to fix these three
problems?

Also, the _stove_ 5. in Apartment 3A is _broken_ 6. . The
tenants can't use it. Would you please call a repair person?

The _carpet_ 7. in Apartment 6A is _stained_ 8. . You need
to clean it.

You need to fix these problems right away. Your tenants are upset. Please call me at (825) 555-1574. Thank you for your attention.

Sincerely,

C. M. Valdez

Claire Valdez
Apartment 5C

1 **Read the questions. Look at the invoice. Fill in the correct answers.**

Travis Carpet Cleaning

4830 Avenue Montague
Montreal, Canada H4L 3Y2
(514) 555-5432 Fax: (514) 555-5433

Commercial and Residential
We keep you clean!

Invoice# 5554

Date: _4/16/13_

Technician: _Lisa Travis_

Payment: ❑ cash ❑ check ☒ credit card

Customer: _Mikey Morin_

Customer: address: _42 Avenue Brentwood, Montreal_

Customer telephone: _(514) 555-5952_

Description of work	Amount
1. Clean dirty carpet in living room, bedroom, and hall	$74.99 (three-room special)
2. Clean dirty carpet in extra bedroom	$45.50
3. Extra work on stained carpet in hall	$25.00

Total: $145.49

1. How much was the three-room special?
   - Ⓐ $25.00
   - Ⓑ $45.50
   - ● $74.99
   - Ⓓ $145.49

2. Where was the stained carpet?
   - ● in the hall
   - Ⓑ in the bedroom
   - Ⓒ in the extra bedroom
   - Ⓓ in the living room

3. How much is the total?
   - Ⓐ $25.00
   - Ⓑ $45.50
   - Ⓒ $74.99
   - ● $145.49

4. Who is the customer?
   - Ⓐ Lisa Travis
   - ● Mikey Morin
   - Ⓒ Montague
   - Ⓓ Travis Carpet Cleaning

5. How did the customer pay?
   - Ⓐ with cash
   - Ⓑ by check
   - ● by credit card
   - Ⓓ none of the above

6. What is the customer's telephone number?
   - Ⓐ (514) 555-5432
   - Ⓑ (514) 555-5433
   - Ⓒ (514) 555-5554
   - ● (514) 555-5952

Check your answers. See page 141.

2 Complete the conversation about the new apartment. Use *let's* and *let's not* with *buy*, *make*, *fix*, or *clean*.

1. **A** The window is broken.

   B _____Let's fix_____ it.

   A OK, _____let's fix_____ it.

2. **A** The couch is stained.

   B I know. _____ a new couch.

   A No, _____ a new one. It's too expensive. _____
   it ourselves. I have a special cleaner for couch material.

3. **A** The curtains are torn.

   B _____ new curtains.

   A No, _____ new curtains. _____ new curtains.
   I have some beautiful material.

4. **A** That chair has a broken leg.

   B Yes. _____ a new chair.

   A OK. _____ two new chairs!

5. **A** The carpet is stained.

   B I know. _____ it ourselves.

   A Good idea. _____ some carpet cleaner.

Check your answers. See page 141.   **UNIT 9 113**

LESSON **A** Listening

1 **Look at the picture. Write the words.**

balloons	a card	a guest	a piece of cake
a cake	flowers	perfume	a present

1. _____ *balloons* _____

2. _____

7. _____

5. _____

3. _____

6. _____

8. _____

4. _____

Check your answers. See page 141.

2 Find the words.

balloons	card	graduation	party	piece
cake	flowers	guest	perfume	present

g	p	a	r	t	y	p	p	p
r	r	e	t	a	e	g	s	i
a	e	p	a	y	u	u	b	e
d	s	i	c	g	p	e	a	c
u	e	c	a	k	e	s	l	e
a	n	b	r	s	r	t	l	p
t	t	n	d	a	f	i	o	a
i	e	r	f	s	u	n	o	f
o	u	c	y	l	m	t	n	t
n	f	l	o	w	e	r	s	a

3 Listen. Circle T (True) or F (False).

TRACK 34

Conversation A

1. Amy is having a graduation party.   (T)   F
2. Amy's dad made the cake.   T   F
3. Uncle Lee brought Amy some perfume.   T   F

Conversation B

4. Ms. Landers is Amy's teacher.   T   F
5. Uncle Lee is playing with his children.   T   F
6. Amy is going to get the children some water.   T   F

Conversation C

7. Sophie is Amy's sister.   T   F
8. Amy's sister is at the party.   T   F
9. Danny's card is funny.   T   F

Check your answers. See page 141.

LESSON B Would you like some cake?

Study the chart on page 130.

1 Read the answers. Write the questions.

1. **A** _Would you like some cake?_
   some cake

   B Yes, I would.

2. **A** _____
   some coffee

   B Yes, they would.

3. **A** _____
   some ice cream

   B Yes, we would.

4. **A** _____
   a balloon

   B Yes, she would.

5. **A** _____
   some flowers

   B Yes, they would.

6. **A** _____
   some dessert

   B Yes, I would.

7. **A** _____
   a cup of tea

   B Yes, he would.

2 Read the questions. Circle the answers.

1. **A** Would you like some cake?

   B a. Yes, I would.

   b. I'd like some cake.

2. **A** What would you like?

   B a. Yes, please.

   b. I'd like some coffee, please.

3. **A** Would they like a cup of tea?

   B a. No, they wouldn't.

   b. No, I don't.

4. **A** What would she like?

   B a. She'd like it.

   b. She'd like a sandwich.

5. **A** Would they like some ice cream?

   B a. Yes, they would.

   b. They would like some soda.

6. **A** What would he like to drink?

   B a. He'd like some soda, please.

   b. Yes, he would.

7. **A** Would you like some coffee?

   B a. He'd like water, and I'd like tea.

   b. Yes, we would.

8. **A** What would you like to eat?

   B a. No, thank you.

   b. I'd like a piece of cake.

Check your answers. See page 141.

3 Look at the pictures. Complete the conversations.

1. **A** What would your friends like to drink?

   B *They'd like some soda.*

2. **A** Would your husband like something to drink?

   B Yes, please. _____

3. **A** What would you and your husband like to eat?

   B _____

4. **A** Would your daughter like a sandwich?

   B No, thanks. But _____.

5. **A** Would you like something to eat?

   B Yes, please. _____

6. **A** Would you like something to drink?

   B No, thanks. But _____.

4 Listen and write the words to complete the conversation.

TRACK 35

LARRY Welcome to Sarah's graduation party! _____*What would you*_____ like to drink?
                                                                1.

SUSIE _____ some soda, please.
                  2.

LARRY _____ a piece of cake, too?
                  3.

SUSIE No, _____. I'm full.
                   4.

LARRY OK. How about you, Jerry? _____ something to drink?
                                                       5.

JERRY Yes, thank you. _____ a cup of tea, please.
                               6.

LARRY OK. Here you go. _____ something to eat?
                                 7.

JERRY Yes, please. _____ a hot dog, a sandwich, some
                           8.
cookies, and two pieces of cake.

LARRY Wow! OK. How about your children? _____ like to eat?
                                                          9.

JERRY My children? This food is for them!

Check your answers. See page 141.

LESSON C Tim gave Mary a present.

Study the chart on page 130.

1 Rewrite the sentences.

1. Tim gave a present to Mary.

   Tim gave Mary a present.

2. Jim bought some flowers for Sarah.

   _____

3. Elias wrote an e-mail to his father.

   _____

4. Marta bought some soda for her son.

   _____

5. Felix gave some ice cream to his children.

   _____

6. Liu-na sent a birthday card to her mother.

   _____

2 Answer the questions. Use *her*, *him*, or *them*.

1. *A* What did Tim give Mary?

   B *Tim gave her a present.*

2. *A* What did Jim buy Sarah?

   B _____

3. *A* What did Elias write his father?

   B _____

4. *A* What did Marta buy her son?

   B _____

5. *A* What did Felix give his children?

   B _____

6. *A* What did Liu-na send her mother?

   B _____

Check your answers. See pages 141–142.

3 Read the list of Mick and Mina's wedding presents. Complete the conversation.

Gift	From	Thank-you note
a check	Mina's parents	✓
a barbecue grill	Mick's brother	
a salad bowl	Maria	✓
coffee cups	Penny	
linens	Rod	
towels	Mina's sister	✓

MICK Would you like some help?

MINA Yes, please. Could you write a thank-you note to your brother?

MICK OK. What did he give us?

MINA He gave us a ___barbecue grill___.
1.

MICK Oh, that's right. OK. What about Maria? What did she give us?

MINA She gave us _____. But don't write her a thank-you note
2.

because I already wrote one. Could you write Rod a note?

MICK Sure. Did he give us the _____?
3.

MINA Yes. Did Penny give us the _____?
4.

MICK Yeah. They're nice! And look, your parents gave us _____.
5.

4 Answer the questions. Use them.

1. Who gave Mick and Mina a check?
   Mina's parents gave them a check.

2. Who gave Mick and Mina coffee cups?
   _____

3. What did Maria give Mick and Mina?
   _____

4. What did Mina's sister give Mick and Mina?
   _____

LESSON D Reading

1 Read and answer the questions about the e-mail. Then listen.

TRACK 36

From: Do-cheon Yoon <dyoon13@cup.org>

To: Chi-ho Yoon <chyoon42@cup.org>

Date: November 1, 2013

Subject: Halloween

Hi Dad,

How are you? We're all great here. Last night was Halloween. Halloween is the children's favorite holiday. It was a lot of fun. The children made their own costumes. I took the children "trick-or-treating," and Yuni stayed home to give out candy. Over a hundred children came to our house for candy! After we got home, our children ate some candy, and then they went to bed. It will probably take about a month to eat all the candy!

Love,

Do-cheon

1. What is the children's favorite holiday? *Halloween.* _____

2. When was Halloween? _____

3. Who made the children's costumes? _____

4. Who went "trick-or-treating" with the children? _____

5. What did Yuni do? _____

6. How long will it take to eat all the candy? _____

2 Match the celebrations with the items.

1. Thanksgiving _d_   a. white dress
2. a wedding ____   b. presents for mothers
3. Valentine's Day ____   c. presents for a house
4. New Year's Eve ____   d. turkey for dinner
5. Mother's Day ____   e. barbecues and fireworks
6. a baby shower ____   f. candy and costumes for children
7. a housewarming ____   g. parties until midnight
8. Halloween ____   h. presents for babies
9. Independence Day ____   i. chocolates, flowers, and cards with red hearts

Check your answers. See page 142.

3 Read the sentences. What was the celebration?

1. I wore a beautiful white dress. There were flowers everywhere.
   People gave us beautiful presents. _A wedding._

2. We went to my grandmother's house. She cooked us a big
   turkey dinner. _____

3. The children went to all the houses in the neighborhood. The neighbors
   gave them candy. _____

4. Last Sunday, my children brought me breakfast in bed. _____

5. We went to a big party. At midnight we celebrated. We went home
   at 1:00 a.m. _____

6. People gave us clothes and toys for our new baby. _____

4 Complete the chart. Use some celebrations more than once.

| a baby shower | Independence Day | New Year's Eve | Valentine's Day |
| a housewarming | Mother's Day | Thanksgiving | a wedding |

Parties	No school or work	Give presents or cards
a baby shower		a baby shower

Check your answers. See page 142.

LESSON E Writing

1 Write sentences.

1. the / for / interesting / you / Thank you / book / me / gave / .

   Thank you for the interesting book you gave me.

2. reading / excited / really / I'm / it / about / .

   I'm really excited about reading it

3. Thank you / for / cake / to / party / bringing / a / our / .

   Thank you for bringing a cake to our party

4. really / I / liked / a lot / it / .

   I really liked a lot it.

5. to / coming / for / Thank you / my / party / graduation / .

   Thank you for coming to my graduation party

6. you / hope / I / good / had / time / a / .

   I hope you had a good time.

2 Complete the thank-you note. Use the sentences from Exercise 1.

June 15, 2013

Dear Erica,

_____Thank you for the interesting book you gave me_____.

I'm really excited about reading it. It looks really good.
1.

Also, Thank you for bringing a cake to our party.
2.

I really like a lot it. Chocolate is my favorite kind of cake!
3.

Thank you for coming to my graduation party
4.

I hope you had a good time. I had a very
5.

good time! I hope to see you soon.
6.

Sincerely,
Joe

Check your answers. See page 142.

3 Answer the questions. Use the information from Exercises 1 and 2.

1. Whose party was it?

   It was Joe's party.

2. When did Joe write the thank-you note?

   He wrote the note on June 15. 2013

3. Who did Joe write the thank-you note to?

   He wrote the note to Erica

4. What did Erica give Joe?

   Erica give a book

5. What did Erica bring to the party?

   Erica brought a cake.

6. Why did Joe like the cake?

   Joe liked the chocolete cake. because it was his favorito flavor. favorite.

4 Read the story. Complete the thank-you note.

chocolates   Dan   favorite   hope   Thank you   Valentine's Day

Dan visited Leanne on Valentine's Day. He gave Leanne a box of chocolates. They were Leanne's favorite kind of candy. She wrote him a note two days later.

February 16, 2013

Dear ____Dan____,
1.

Thank you for the chocalates you gave me for valentine's day
2.   3.

They were delicious! They are my favorite kind.
4.

Thank you so much for visiting me on Valentine's Day.
5.

I hope you had fun.
6.

Sincerely,
Leanne

1 **Read the questions. Look at the invitation. Fill in the correct answers.**

1. What is this?
   ● It's an e-mail invitation.
   Ⓑ It's an e-mail thank-you card.
   Ⓒ It's a paper invitation.
   Ⓓ It's an RSVP to an invitation.

2. When is the party?
   Ⓐ April 12
   Ⓑ April 14
   ● April 15
   Ⓓ April 18

3. What kind of party is it?
   ● a birthday party
   Ⓑ a children's party
   Ⓒ a graduation party
   Ⓓ a lunch party

4. How long is the party?
   Ⓐ four hours
   ● five hours
   Ⓒ six hours
   Ⓓ seven hours

5. How many guests are coming?
   Ⓐ 0
   Ⓑ 5
   ● 25
   Ⓓ 30

6. Who is giving the party?
   Ⓐ Cristal Sheila
   ● Paco Cristal
   Ⓒ Cristal Paco
   Ⓓ Sheila Cristal

7. What should people bring to the party?
   ● something to barbecue
   Ⓑ something to drink
   Ⓒ flowers and gifts
   Ⓓ all of the above

8. When do people need to say yes or no?
   Ⓐ by 4/12
   ● by 4/14
   Ⓒ by 4/15
   Ⓓ by 12/4

Check your answers. See page 142.

2 Complete the sentences about the pictures. Use *there is*, *there isn't any*, *there are*, *there aren't any*, *there was*, *there wasn't any*, *there were*, and *there weren't any*.

Mom's graduation party – 1993

1. _____*There were*_____ six people at the party.
2. _____There was_____ a small cake on the table.
3. _____There were_____ flowers on the table.
4. _____There was_____ fruit on the table.
5. _There wasn't any_ ice cream on the table.
6. _There were'nt any_ balloons on the table.

My graduation party – Today

7. _____*There are*_____ twelve people at the party.
8. _There is_____ a large cake on the table.
9. _There aren't any_ flowers on the table.
10. _There isn't any_ fruit on the table.
11. _There is_____ ice cream on the table.
12. _There are_____ balloons on the table.

Check your answers. See page 142.

Reference

Present continuous

Use the present continuous for actions happening now and in the near future.

Wh- questions

What	am	I	doing now?
	are	you	
	is	he	
	is	she	
	is	it	
	are	we	
	are	you	
	are	they	

Answers

You're	working.
I'm	
He's	
She's	
It's	
You're	
We're	
They're	

Contractions

I'm	=	I am
You're	=	You are
He's	=	He is
She's	=	She is
It's	=	It is
We're	=	We are
You're	=	You are
They're	=	They are

Simple present

Use the simple present for repeated, usual, or daily actions.

Yes / No questions

Do	I	work?
Do	you	
Does	he	
Does	she	
Does	it	
Do	we	
Do	you	
Do	they	

Short answers

Yes,	you	do.
	I	do.
	he	does.
	she	does.
	it	does.
	you	do.
	we	do.
	they	do.

No,	you	don't.
	I	don't.
	he	doesn't.
	she	doesn't.
	it	doesn't.
	you	don't.
	we	don't.
	they	don't.

Wh- questions: What

What	do	I	do every day?
	do	you	
	does	he	
	does	she	
	does	it	
	do	we	
	do	you	
	do	they	

Answers

You		work.
I		work.
He		works.
She	usually	works.
It		works.
You		work.
We		work.
They		work.

Wh- questions: When

When	do	I	usually work?
	do	you	
	does	he	
	does	she	
	do	we	
	do	you	
	do	they	

Answers

You		work	on Friday.
I		work	
He		works	
She	usually	works	
You		work	
We		work	
They		work	

Simple present of *want* and *need*

Wh- questions: *What*

What	do	I	want	to do?
	do	you		
	does	he		
	does	she		
	do	we		
	do	you		
	do	they		
What	do	I	need	to do?
	do	you		
	does	he		
	does	she		
	do	we		
	do	you		
	do	they		

Answers

You	want	to go home.
I	want	
He	wants	
She	wants	
You	want	
We	want	
They	want	
You	need	to go home.
I	need	
He	needs	
She	needs	
You	need	
We	need	
They	need	

Simple present of *have to* + verb

Wh- questions: *What*

What	do	I	have to	do?
	do	you		
	does	he		
	does	she		
	does	it		
	do	we		
	do	you		
	do	they		

Answers

You	have to	go home.
I	have to	
He	has to	
She	has to	
It	has to	
You	have to	
We	have to	
They	have to	

Simple present with *Which* questions

Wh- questions: *Which*

Which plumber	do	I	recommend?
	do	you	
	does	he	
	does	she	
	does	it	
	do	we	
	do	you	
	do	they	

Answers

You	recommend	Joe's Plumbing.
I	recommend	
He	recommends	
She	recommends	
It	recommends	
You	recommend	
We	recommend	
They	recommend	

Simple past with regular and irregular verbs

Use the simple past for actions completed in the past.

Wh- questions: What

What	did	I / you / he / she / it / we / you / they	do?

Affirmative statements

I / You / He / She / It / We / You / They	stayed. / ate.

Negative statements

I / You / He / She / It / We / You / They	didn't	stay. / eat.

didn't = did not

Yes / No questions

Did	I / you / he / she / it / we / you / they	stay? / eat?

Short answers

Yes,	you / I / he / she / it / you / we / they	did.

No,	you / I / he / she / it / you / we / they	didn't.

Wh- questions: When

When	did	I / you / he / she / it / we / you / they	move? / leave?

Answers

You / I / He / She / It / You / We / They	moved / left	last week.

Wh- questions: Where

Where	did	I / you / he / she / it / we / you / they	go?

Answers

You / I / He / She / It / You / We / They	stayed / went	home.

Future with *will*

Use *will* for a prediction or promise in the future.

Wh- questions: *What*

What	will	I you he she we you they	do	tomorrow?

Affirmative statements

I'll You'll He'll She'll We'll You'll They'll	probably	work.

'll = will

Negative statements

I You He She We You They	won't	work.

won't = will not

Future with *be going to*

Use *be going to* for a plan or prediction in the future.

Wh- questions

What	am are is is are are are	I you he she we you they	going to do tomorrow?

Affirmative statements

I'm You're He's She's We're You're They're	going to	play soccer.

Negative statements

I'm You're He's She's We're You're They're	not going to	play soccer.

Should

Wh- questions: *What*

What	should	I you he she we you they	do?

Affirmative statements

I You He She We You They	should	take medicine.

Negative statements

I You He She We You They	shouldn't	take medicine.

shouldn't = should not

Would you like . . . ?

Yes / No questions

Would	you / he / she / you / they	like	some cake?

Short answers

Yes,	I / he / she / we / they	would.

Wh- questions: *What*

What	would	you / he / she / you / they	like?

Answers

I'd / He'd / She'd / We'd / They'd	like	some cake.

'd = would

Direct and indirect objects

Tim gave a present to	me. / you. / him. / her. / Mary. / it. / us. / you. / them.

Tim gave	me / you / him / her / Mary / it / us / you / them	a present.

Simple past irregular verbs

be	→ was / were	eat	→ ate	know	→ knew	sit	→ sat
become	→ became	fall	→ fell	leave	→ left	sleep	→ slept
begin	→ began	feel	→ felt	lose	→ lost	speak	→ spoke
break	→ broke	fight	→ fought	make	→ made	spend	→ spent
bring	→ brought	find	→ found	meet	→ met	stand	→ stood
build	→ built	fly	→ flew	pay	→ paid	steal	→ stole
buy	→ bought	forget	→ forgot	put	→ put	swim	→ swam
catch	→ caught	give	→ gave	read	→ read	take	→ took
choose	→ chose	go	→ went	ride	→ rode	teach	→ taught
come	→ came	have	→ had	run	→ ran	tell	→ told
cost	→ cost	hear	→ heard	say	→ said	think	→ thought
cut	→ cut	hide	→ hid	see	→ saw	understand	→ understood
do	→ did	hold	→ held	sell	→ sold	wake	→ woke
drink	→ drank	hurt	→ hurt	send	→ sent	wear	→ wore
drive	→ drove	keep	→ kept	sing	→ sang	write	→ wrote

Comparative and superlative adjectives

	Adjective	Comparative	Superlative
Adjectives with one syllable	cheap large long new nice old short small tall young	cheaper larger longer newer nicer older shorter smaller taller younger	the cheapest the largest the longest the newest the nicest the oldest the shortest the smallest the tallest the youngest
Adjectives with one syllable ending in a vowel-consonant pair	big fat hot sad	bigger fatter hotter sadder	the biggest the fattest the hottest the saddest
Adjectives with two or more syllables	beautiful comfortable crowded expensive	more beautiful more comfortable more crowded more expensive	the most beautiful the most comfortable the most crowded the most expensive
Adjectives ending in -y	friendly heavy pretty	friendlier heavier prettier	the friendliest the heaviest the prettiest
Irregular adjectives	good bad	better worse	the best the worst

Adjective word order

Size	Age	Shape	Color	Pattern
big large long medium short small	modern new old	curly oval round square straight	black blue brown green purple red white yellow	checked plaid polka dotted striped

Examples

He's wearing a modern purple and yellow striped tie.
She has a large square brown coffee table.
They have a medium-sized old green car.

Answer key

Welcome

Exercise 1A page 2
1. is reading
2. is using
3. is talking
4. are writing
5. is helping

Exercise 1B page 2
1. No, she isn't
2. Yes, he is
3. No, she isn't
4. No, they aren't
5. Yes, she is
6. Yes, he is

Exercise 2A page 3
1. False; Ivan can't cook.
2. True
3. False; Ivan and Irma can't speak Chinese.
4. True
5. False; Joe can't swim.
6. True
7. False; Oscar and Lara can't use a computer.
8. False; Irma can drive a truck.

Exercise 2B page 3
speak English, speak Chinese, write Chinese, cook

Exercise 3A page 4
1. is
2. am
3. is
4. is
5. are
6. is
7. is
8. were
9. weren't
10. were
11. are
12. are
13. was
14. am
15. was
16. is
17. are
18. are

Exercise 3B page 4
1. My name is Diego. I am from Mexico. I was a truck driver in Mexico. I am married. There are five people in my family.
2. My name is Bae. I am from Korea. I was a student in Korea. I am not married. There are two people in my family.
3. My name is Malik. I am from Somalia. I was a cook in Somalia. I am married. There are six people in my family.

Exercise 4A page 5
1. work
2. went
3. goes
4. came
5. had
6. went
7. worked
8. didn't go
9. take
10. slept
11. didn't take
12. walked
13. visit
14. go
15. went
16. celebrated

Exercise 4B page 5
1. slept
2. works
3. takes
4. visited
5. walked
6. went
7. celebrates
8. didn't buy

Unit 1: Personal information

Lesson A: Listening

Exercise 1 page 6
1. curly hair
2. short brown hair
3. a jogging suit
4. striped pants
5. short blond hair
6. long brown hair
7. a white T-shirt
8. a long skirt

Exercise 2 page 6
1. curly hair
2. striped pants
3. short blond hair
4. a white T-shirt
5. short brown hair
6. a jogging suit
7. long brown hair
8. a long skirt

Exercise 3 page 7
Hair color
black
blond
brown
Hair length
long
short
Hair type
curly
straight

Exercise 4 page 7
1. b
2. a
3. a
4. c
5. a
6. c

Lesson B: She's wearing a short plaid skirt.

Exercise 1 page 8
1. a green and white striped dress
2. a black and blue checked shirt
3. a long blue coat
4. small red and yellow shoes
5. black plaid pants
6. short brown boots

Exercise 2 page 8
1. a long blue coat
2. small white and black shoes
3. short brown boots
4. black plaid pants
5. a black and blue checked shirt
6. a green and white striped dress

Exercise 3 page 9
1. a
2. c
3. b
4. c
5. a
6. b

Exercise 4 page 9
Colors	Sizes
black	large
green	long
purple	short
red	small

Clothing
coat
jeans
pants
sweater

Lesson C: What are you doing right now?

Exercise 1 page 10
1. b
2. a
3. b
4. a
5. a
6. b

Exercise 2 page 10
1A. do, do
1B. study
1A. are, doing
1B. am reading
2A. is, doing
2B. is playing
2A. does, do
2B. plays
3A. does, do
3B. works
3A. is, doing
3B. is watching

Exercise 3 page 11

1. a   3. b   5. a
2. a   4. b   6. b

Exercise 4 page 11

1. leaves   4. talk
2. goes   5. sits
3. calls   6. studies

Exercise 5 page 11

1. is relaxing
2. is watching
3. are sitting
4. is drinking
5. is wearing
6. is speaking

Lesson D: Reading

Exercise 1 page 12

Present continuous
am writing
are working
am wearing

Simple present
think   go
miss   wears
is   goes

Exercise 2 page 12

1. She's in the lunchroom.
2. She lives in Chicago.
3. She lives in New York.
4. He wears a uniform.
5. She wears jeans.
6. She's writing an e-mail.

Exercise 3 page 13

```
t f d b a w t o m d e a
e t g l o v e s d n a v
t n p c b e x u a p r p
i z z h a t a n c l r w
a n y r d o b g v m i a
n t d g m b e l p b n t
a p u r s e l a e h g c
x v r s k f t s s t s h
d v i n t i e s c a r f
h b n b r a c e l e t p
r a g i k j j s q w w c
t n e c k l a c e d d i
```

Exercise 4 page 13

1. earrings   7. purse
2. scarf   8. hat
3. necklace   9. sunglasses
4. belt   10. tie
5. bracelet   11. watch
6. ring   12. gloves

Lesson E: Writing

Exercise 1 page 14

A

1. green   5. jacket
2. goes   6. earrings
3. visits   7. Norma
4. watches

B

1. brown   4. goes
2. white   5. plays
3. jeans   6. Sarah

C

1. wearing   5. goes
2. shoes   6. studies
3. blond   7. Martina
4. blue

Exercise 2 page 15

1. Bobby goes to New York City on the weekend.
2. Georgia is wearing a black scarf and a red coat.
3. Susana goes to work after school every Monday.
4. Mei's hair is long.
5. Martin is carrying his books in a backpack.
6. Christina is wearing a watch.

Exercise 3 page 15

1. On the weekend, Mary teaches English.
2. Sam leaves early every night.
3. Alberto watches TV on Thursday.
4. On Saturday, Raquel plays soccer.
5. Every Sunday, Michael wears a suit.
6. Petra has a birthday party every June.

Lesson F: Another view

Exercise 1 page 16

1. C   3. D   5. C
2. C   4. A   6. B

Exercise 2, page 17

1. and Dan does, too
2. and Rob doesn't, either
3. but Rachel doesn't
4. and Rob does, too
5. and Luke doesn't, either
6. but Alicia doesn't
7. and Luke does, too
8. and Alicia doesn't, either
9. but Dan doesn't
10. and Rachel doesn't, either

Unit 2: At school

Lesson A: Listening

Exercise 1 page 18

1. a computer lab   5. a student
2. a lab instructor 6. a mouse
3. a monitor   7. a keyboard
4. a hall

Exercise 2 page 18

1. keyboarding   4. work
2. instructor   5. skill
3. computer   6. register

Exercise 3 page 19

1. Diego's English teacher.
2. Diego's computer lab teacher.
3. 555-23-0967.
4. Room H102.
5. MW 6:00–7:50 p.m.
6. Computer lab.

Exercise 4 page 19

1. F   4. F   7. T
2. T   5. F   8. T
3. F   6. T   9. F

Lesson B: What do you want to do?

Exercise 1 page 20

1. f   3. d   5. c
2. e   4. b   6. a

Exercise 2 page 20

1. needs to take
2. wants to go
3. wants to get
4. want to talk
5. need to learn
6. need to register

Exercise 3 page 21

1. He needs to take an auto mechanics class.
2. She needs to take a driver education class.
3. You need to take a citizenship class.
4. He needs to go to Room 131.
5. I need to go to Room 231.
6. They need to take a computer technology class.

Lesson C: What will you do?

Exercise 1 page 22

1. will   4. will
2. will   5. won't
3. won't   6. will

Exercise 2 page 22

1. He'll work on Thursday.
2. He'll take a driving lesson on Tuesday.
3. He'll work on Friday.
4. He'll meet Lisa for lunch on Saturday.
5. He'll call his mother on Sunday.
6. He'll take an English class on Monday and Wednesday.

Exercise 3 page 23

1. buy a house
2. go to the U.S.
3. open a business
4. study English
5. get a GED
6. take a vocational course

Exercise 4 page 23

1. What will she do in five years?
2. What will he do next year?
3. What will you do tomorrow?
4. What will they do this weekend?

Lesson D: Reading

Exercise 1 page 24

1. 18 months.
2. On March 14.
3. At City College.
4. Registration, the classes, and the certificate.
5. Teachers and current students.

Exercise 2 page 24

1. b   2. c   3. c   4. a

Exercise 3 page 25

1. e   3. a   5. c
2. d   4. b

Exercise 4 page 25

1. computer networking
2. dental assisting
3. fitness training
4. criminal justice
5. veterinary assisting
6. nail care
7. home health care
8. counseling

Lesson E: Writing

Exercise 1 page 26

1. b   3. f   5. c
2. d   4. a   6. e

Exercise 2 page 26

1. get a second job on the weekend
2. he has a new baby
3. talk to people about job possibilities

4. read the classified section of the newspaper
5. look for jobs online
6. two months

Exercise 3 page 27

1. goal   4. Second
2. children   5. Third
3. First   6. year

Exercise 4 page 27

1. She wants to help her children with their homework.
2. She needs to find an adult school.
3. She needs to practice her English every day.
4. She needs to volunteer with the Parent-Teacher Association (PTA) at her children's school.
5. She will be ready next year.

Lesson F: Another view

Exercise 1 page 28

1. B   3. A   5. D
2. D   4. C   6. B

Exercise 2 page 29

1. I'm going to study at the library.
2. I'm having chicken.
3. I'm going to watch TV.
4. I'll get up at 6:00 a.m.
5. I'm registering for a class.
6. I'll take Criminal Justice 2.
7. I'm visiting friends.
8. I'll swim and hike.
9. I'm going to get a job.
10. I'm taking flowers.

Unit 3: Friends and family

Lesson A: Listening

Exercise 1 page 30

1. smoke
2. groceries
3. broken-down car
4. overheated engine
5. worried man
6. trunk
7. hood

Exercise 2 page 30

1. overheated engine
2. smoke
3. worried man
4. hood
5. groceries
6. trunk
7. broken-down car

Exercise 3 page 31

1. worried   5. smoke
2. broke   6. engine
3. groceries   7. hood
4. trunk

Lesson B: What did you do last weekend?

Exercise 1 page 32

1. b   3. b   5. a
2. a   4. b   6. a

Exercise 2 page 32

1. grilled   7. had
2. bought   8. watched
3. drove   9. met
4. ate   10. played
5. fixed   11. read
6. went   12. stayed

Exercise 3 page 33

1. went   4. had
2. met   5. ate
3. played   6. drove

Exercise 4 page 33

a. 5   c. 3   e. 1
b. 2   d. 4   f. 6

Lesson C: When do you usually play soccer?

Exercise 1 page 34

1. went   4. eats
2. watch   5. leave
3. cleaned   6. met

Exercise 2 page 34

1. d   3. e   5. f   7. a
2. g   4. b   6. c   8. h

Exercise 3 page 35

1. has   5. met
2. plays   6. gets
3. worked   7. eat
4. has   8. ate

Exercise 4 page 35

1. They usually buy groceries on Thursday.
2. She took her English exam on Friday.
3. He usually meets his friends after work.
4. She went to a movie with her uncle on Monday.
5. He met his friends at 5:30.
6. He studied for an English test.

Lesson D: Reading

Exercise 1 page 36

1. d   3. b   5. a   7. a
2. c   4. d   6. d   8. a

Exercise 2 page 37
1. the laundry
2. the dishes
3. lunch
4. the bed
5. a bath
6. a nap
7. dressed
8. up

Exercise 3 page 37
1. make
2. got
3. do
4. do
5. did
6. did
7. do
8. takes

Lesson E: Writing
Exercise 1 page 38
1. Ana usually gets up first.
2. Ron got up first this morning.
3. Ana usually takes a bath every morning.
4. Ana didn't take a bath this morning.
5. Ed usually leaves for work at 7:20.
6. The children usually leave for school at 7:30.

Exercise 2 page 39
1. She gets up at 6:00.
2. She gets dressed at 6:15.
3. She eats her breakfast at 7:10.
4. She does the dishes at 7:45.
5. She makes the children's beds at 7:15.
6. She leaves the house at 7:55.

Exercise 3 page 39
1. Next, First, Finally
2. Finally, First, Next

Exercise 4 page 39
1. Last Monday, I had a very bad morning. First, I woke up late. Next, I didn't have time for breakfast. Finally, I was late for work.
2. Last Sunday, my family went to the beach. First, we had a picnic lunch. Next, we relaxed all afternoon. Finally, we drove home for dinner.

Lesson F: Another view
Exercise 1 page 40
1. C
2. D
3. A
4. B
5. C
6. D

Exercise 2 page 41
1. makes cookies
2. plays cards
3. cooks dinner
4. do housework
5. go dancing
6. make breakfast

7. plays soccer
8. goes shopping
9. does homework
10. plays basketball
11. does chores
12. plays computer games

Unit 4: Health
Lesson A: Listening
Exercise 1 page 42
1. injured hand
2. crutches
3. sprained ankle
4. broken bone
5. inhaler
6. X-ray
7. painful knee

Exercise 2 page 42
1. X-ray
2. broken bone
3. injured hand
4. inhaler
5. crutches
6. painful knee
7. sprained ankle

Exercise 3 page 43
1. sprained
2. crutches
3. injured
4. X-ray
5. broken
6. inhaler

Exercise 4 page 43
1. b
2. b
3. a
4. c
5. a
6. c

Lesson B: You should go to the hospital.
Exercise 1 page 44
1. should
2. shouldn't
3. shouldn't
4. should
5. should
6. shouldn't

Exercise 2 page 44
1. shouldn't, should
2. shouldn't, should
3. should, shouldn't
4. shouldn't, should
5. should, shouldn't
6. should, shouldn't

Exercise 3 page 45
1. clothes
2. break
3. water
4. towel
5. sun
6. shade

Exercise 4 page 45
1. should
2. shouldn't
3. should
4. should
5. should
6. shouldn't

Lesson C: You have to see a doctor.
Exercise 1 page 46
1. has to
2. has to
3. have to

4. have to
5. has to
6. have to

Exercise 2 page 46
1. He has to use crutches.
2. She has to see the doctor.
3. He has to get an X-ray.
4. He has to fill out an accident report.
5. She has to take medicine.

Exercise 3 page 47
1. c
2. f
3. d
4. e
5. b
6. a

Exercise 4 page 47
1. prescription
2. do
3. have to
4. medicine
5. refrigerator
6. morning
7. food

Lesson D: Reading
Exercise 1 page 48
1. a
2. b
3. c
4. b
5. d
6. a

Exercise 2 page 49
1. d
2. e
3. b
4. a
5. c

Exercise 3 page 49
1. She has a rash.
2. They have allergies.
3. He has a swollen knee.
4. He has chest pains.
5. She has chills.
6. He has a sprained wrist.

Exercise 4 page 49
1. hurt
2. accident
3. chest
4. cut
5. medicine

Lesson E: Writing
Exercise 1 page 50
1. There were four accidents in August.
2. The waiter had a sprained ankle.
3. The cook burned his hand on August 10.
4. Mr. Engels cut his hand.
5. Ms. Perry had a sprained wrist.
6. The name of the restaurant is Sleepy Burgers.

Exercise 2 page 50
1. 3, 1, 2
2. 2, 1, 3

Exercise 3 page 51
1. burned
2. injuries
3. accident
4. has to
5. medicine
6. days
7. shouldn't
8. work

Exercise 4 page 51
1. Carlos Garcia was hurt.
2. He had burned hands.
3. He was hurt this afternoon / on May 9, 2013.
4. Yes, it was.
5. He can return to work on May 16, 2013.
6. The name of the restaurant is Fast Frank's Restaurant.

Lesson F: Another view
Exercise 1 page 52
1. C   3. D   5. B
2. C   4. C   6. A

Exercise 2 page 52
1. tablets   3. product
2. doctor   4. drowsiness

Exercise 3 page 53
1. d, a, b
2. c, e
3. f

1. have to / must
2. have to / must
3. must not
4. have to / must
5. must not
6. don't have to

Unit 5: Around town
Lesson A: Listening
Exercise 1 page 54
1. a suitcase
2. an information desk
3. a waiting area
4. a track
5. a ticket booth
6. departures
7. arrivals

Exercise 2 page 54
1. a ticket booth
2. a suitcase
3. an information desk
4. a track
5. a waiting area
6. departures
7. arrivals

Exercise 3 page 55
1. b   3. f   5. a
2. d   4. c   6. e

Exercise 4 page 55
1. F   4. F   7. F
2. T   5. T   8. T
3. T   6. F   9. T

Lesson B: How often? How long?
Exercise 1 page 56
1. a   2. a   3. b   4. c

Exercise 2 page 57
1. f   3. b   5. d
2. a   4. e   6. c

Exercise 3 page 57
1. How often do you drive to the beach?
   How long does it take?
2. How often do you walk to the park?
   How long does it take?
3. How often do you go downtown by bus?
   How long does it take?

Lesson C: She often walks to school.
Exercise 1 page 58
1. never   4. often
2. rarely   5. always
3. sometimes

Exercise 2 page 58
1. often   7. sometimes
2. rarely   8. sometimes
3. always   9. rarely
4. never   10. often
5. always   11. often
6. never   12. rarely

Exercise 3 page 59
1. He always walks to school.
2. He never drives to school.
3. He rarely eats lunch at 1:00 p.m.
4. He usually eats dinner at home.
5. He usually goes to sleep at 10:00 p.m.

Exercise 4 page 59
1a. Yes   3a. No
1b. No   3b. Yes
2a. No
2b. Yes

Lesson D: Reading
Exercise 1 page 60
1. c   2. c   3. d   4. b

Exercise 2 page 60
1. Mariam   3. know
2. at a hotel 4. Mariam

Exercise 3 page 61
1. goes   6. buy
2. stays   7. take
3. takes   8. write
4. go   9. stays
5. go

Exercise 4 page 61
6, 3, 2, 8, 5, 1, 7, 4
A How often do you go on vacation?
B I go on vacation once a year.
A Where do you usually go?
B I usually go to Denver to see my parents.
A How long does it take to get there?
B It usually takes about three hours by plane.
A Do you always go by plane?
B Oh, yes! It takes two days by car.

Lesson E: Writing
Exercise 1 page 62
1. How often do trains go to Miami?
2. How long does it take to get to San Francisco?
3. How long does it take to drive to Detroit?
4. How often does the bus go to Boston?
5. How often do you visit your relatives in Houston?
6. Where do you usually stay?

Exercise 2 page 62
a. 5   c. 4   e. 2
b. 1   d. 6   f. 3

Exercise 3 page 62
1. one hour and five minutes
2. one hour and forty-five minutes
3. nine minutes
4. one hour and seven minutes
5. half an hour (or 30 minutes)
6. one hour and twelve minutes

Exercise 4 page 63
1. Every year   3. Rarely
2. One week   4. Very happy

Exercise 5 page 63
1. goes   7. uses
2. takes   8. sleeps
3. leaves   9. takes
4. gets   10. talks
5. doesn't like 11. likes
6. are   12. doesn't like

Lesson F: Another view
Exercise 1 page 64
1. How often does the bus go?
   It goes every half hour.
2. How does Shen-hui get to school?
   Shen-hui gets to school by
   bicycle.
3. How long does it take to get from
   Shen-hui's house to school by
   bicycle?
   It takes 20 minutes.
4. How often does Phillipe
   arrive on time?
   Phillipe always arrives on time.
5. How long does it take to get from
   Sara's house to school
   by subway?
   It takes 22 minutes.
6. How does Zoe get to school?
   Zoe drives to school.

Exercise 2 page 65
1. into	7. out of
2. through	8. through
3. toward	9. toward
4. into	10. into
5. through	11. out of
6. out of	

Unit 6: Time

Lesson A: Listening
Exercise 1 page 66
1. class picture	4. baby
2. family	5. photo album
3. graduation	6. wedding

Exercise 2 page 66
1. photo album	4. wedding
2. graduation	5. class picture
3. family	6. baby

Exercise 3 page 67
1. a	3. b	5. b
2. c	4. c	

Exercise 4 page 67
1. T	4. F	7. T
2. F	5. F	8. T
3. T	6. T	9. F

Lesson B: When did you move here?
Exercise 1 page 68
1. moved	6. started
2. had	7. got
3. began	8. left
4. studied	9. met
5. found	10. graduated

Exercise 2 page 68
Regular verbs
moved
studied
started
graduated
Irregular verbs
had
began
found
got
left
met

Exercise 3 page 68
1. I moved here in 2000.
2. Ken started college in September.
3. We met in 1988.
4. We got married in 1990.
5. They began taking English
   classes last year.
6. Norma left for vacation
   on Saturday.

Exercise 4 page 69
1. When did Elsa meet Pablo?
2. When did they get married?
3. They had Gabriel in 1991.
4. When did they have Clara?
5. They left Guatemala in 1999.
6. They moved from Chicago to
   Detroit in 2001.
7. When did Elsa start taking ESL
   classes?
8. She got her driver's license
   in 2005.

Lesson C: He graduated two years ago.
Exercise 1 page 70
ago
four days
a week
two years
a month
six months
in
the afternoon
December
1999
July
the morning
on
March 23rd
May 9th
Wednesday
April 11th, 1990
Saturday
at
6:15
night
noon
half past four

Exercise 2 page 70
1. last	6. this
2. on	7. before
3. at	8. on
4. ago	9. before
5. in	10. ago

Exercise 3 page 71
1. last	5. in
2. on	6. ago
3. at	7. after
4. before	8. last

Exercise 4 page 71
1. He took his driving test four
   days ago.
2. He shopped for his sister's
   graduation present last week.
3. He played basketball on Friday,
   May 15th.
4. He had a doctor's appointment at
   4:30.
5. He took his books back to the
   library two days ago.

Lesson D: Reading
Exercise 1 page 72
1. immigrated	8. got
2. worked	9. got
3. started	10. found
4. studied	11. started
5. began	12. had
6. met	13. decided
7. fell	

Exercise 2 page 72
1. She immigrated ten years ago.
2. She started English classes after
   she came to the U.S.
3. She studied English for three
   years.
4. They got married three years
   ago.
5. They found jobs after they
   got married.

Exercise 3 page 73
a. 5	c. 4	e. 6
b. 3	d. 1	f. 2

Exercise 4 page 73
1. immigrated
2. fell in love
3. got married
4. got engaged
5. got promoted
6. started a business
7. had a baby
8. retire

Lesson E: Writing
Exercise 1 page 74
1. on
2. had
3. started
4. in
5. took
6. worked
7. In
8. learned
9. After
10. found
11. last
12. opened

Exercise 2 page 74
1. b
2. d
3. f
4. a
5. c
6. e

Exercise 3 page 75
1. On January 5, 2005, she left China.
   She left China on January 5, 2005.
2. In February 2005, she began English classes.
   She began English classes in February 2005.
3. For two years, she took English classes.
   She took English classes for two years.
4. In September 2006, she began vocational school.
   She began vocational school in September 2006.
5. In 2008, she graduated from vocational school.
   She graduated from vocational school in 2008.
6. In September 2008, she found a job as a chef.
   She found a job as a chef in 2008.
7. Last week, she opened her own restaurant.
   She opened her own restaurant last week.

Lesson F: Another view
Exercise 1 page 76
1. B
2. A
3. B
4. A
5. C
6. D

Exercise 2 page 77
1. anyone; no one
2. anyone; everyone
3. anyone; no one
4. anyone; someone
5. anyone someone
6. anyone; everyone

Unit 7: Shopping
Lesson A: Listening
Exercise 1 page 78
1. stove
2. salesperson
3. sofa
4. piano
5. customer
6. appliances
7. furniture
8. price tag

Exercise 2 page 78
1. sofa
2. furniture
3. customer
4. stove
5. salesperson
6. price tag
7. piano
8. appliances

Exercise 3 page 79
1. furniture
2. salesperson
3. customer
4. appliances
5. sofa
6. price tag
7. piano
8. stove

Lesson B: The brown sofa is bigger.
Exercise 1 page 80
1. bigger
2. better
3. heavier
4. more comfortable

Exercise 2 page 80
1. more comfortable
2. prettier
3. more expensive
4. cheaper
5. bigger
6. heavier

Exercise 3 page 81
1. The dining room table is bigger.
2. The red chairs are smaller.
3. The refrigerator is more expensive.
4. The blue desk is older.
5. The green sofa is longer.
6. The black lamp is shorter.

Lesson C: The yellow chair is the cheapest.
Exercise 1 page 82
1. more expensive, the most expensive
2. cheaper, the cheapest
3. friendlier, the friendliest
4. better, the best
5. newer, the newest
6. heavier, the heaviest
7. lower, the lowest
8. more beautiful, the most beautiful
9. prettier, the prettiest
10. more crowded, the most crowded
11. more comfortable, the most comfortable
12. nicer, the nicest

Exercise 2 page 82
1. the lowest
2. the most comfortable
3. the best
4. the most expensive
5. the nicest
6. the prettiest
7. the cheapest
8. the most crowded
9. the heaviest

Exercise 3 page 83
1. a small lamp, a smaller lamp, the smallest lamp
2. an expensive desk, a more expensive desk, the most expensive desk
3. a good TV, a better TV, the best TV

Exercise 4 page 83
1. The evening skirt is the most expensive.
2. The evening skirt is the longest.
3. The jeans skirt is the cheapest.
4. The tennis skirt is the shortest.

Lesson D: Reading
Exercise 1 page 84
1. newest
2. big
3. best
4. beautiful
5. nicest
6. most expensive
7. oldest
8. cheaper
9. cheapest
10. small

Exercise 2 page 84
1. The name of the store is Antique Alley.
2. It opened on May 1st.
3. The most expensive thing was a large mirror.
4. It was $1,300.
5. The cheapest thing was a small lamp.
6. It was $12.95.

Exercise 3 page 85

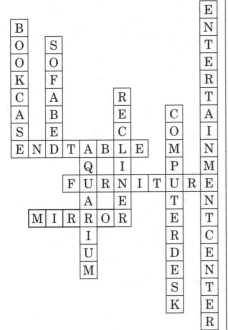

Lesson E: Writing

Exercise 1 page 86
1. The gift is for Miguel.
2. The gift is from his wife Amelia.
3. She gave him an airline ticket.
4. It's his 40th birthday.
5. He will go to Mexico City.
6. He will leave on August 10.

Exercise 2 page 86
1. I bought the red sofa because it was the most comfortable.
2. Sandra gave her sister a pair of earrings because it was her birthday.
3. Mr. and Mrs. Chung shop at the Clothes Corner because it's the nicest store.
4. Roberto bought the brown recliner because it was on sale.
5. I bought an entertainment center because it was 50% off.

Exercise 3 page 87
1. bigger
2. nicer
3. better
4. newer
5. more beautiful
6. higher
7. oldest
8. smallest
9. most crowded

Exercise 4 page 87
1. Super Discounts, the smallest
2. Super Discounts, the oldest
3. Smart Department Store, the biggest
4. Smart Department Store, the most expensive
5. Best Discounts, the cheapest
6. Super Discounts, the most crowded

Lesson F: Another view

Exercise 1 page 88
1. C 3. A 5. C
2. D 4. A 6. B

Exercise 2 page 89
1. One, the other
2. One, the other
3. Some, the others
4. Some, the others
5. Some, the others
6. Some, the others
7. One, the other
8. One, the other
9. One, the other
10. One, the other

Unit 8: Work

Lesson A: Listening

Exercise 1 page 90
1. lab
2. orderly
3. co-workers
4. walker
5. linens
6. patient
7. supplies
8. wheelchair

Exercise 2 page 90
1. lab
2. co-workers
3. linens
4. supplies
5. wheelchair
6. walker
7. orderly
8. patient

Exercise 3 page 91
1. patient
2. co-workers
3. linens
4. wheelchair
5. orderly
6. walker

Exercise 4 page 91
1. T 4. F 7. F
2. F 5. F 8. T
3. F 6. T 9. T

Lesson B: Where did you go last night?

Exercise 1 page 92
1. c 3. b 5. a 7. f
2. e 4. g 6. d

Exercise 2 page 92
1. What
2. Where
3. What
4. What
5. Where
6. What
7. What
8. Where

Exercise 3 page 93
1A. What
1B. They met new patients in the reception area.
2A. Where
2B. She took her patient to the lab.
3A. What
3B. He picked up X-rays from the lab.
4A. What
4B. made the bed in Room 304, delivered X-rays to the doctors.
5A. Where
5B. Jorge went to Room 310.
6A. What
6B. He helped a patient.
7A. What
7B. She took patients from the lab to their rooms.
8A. Where
8B. She went to the fourth floor.
9A. What
9B. He prepared rooms on the second floor.
10A. Where
10B. They went to the cafeteria.

Lesson C: I work on Saturdays and Sundays.

Exercise 1 page 94
1. and
2. or
3. but
4. and
5. but
6. or
7. and
8. and

Exercise 2 page 94
1. Jun eats lunch at noon or at 1:00.
2. Javier helps the nurses and the doctors.
3. Tien picks up the supplies at the warehouse, but she doesn't deliver them.
4. Rieko met her new co-workers this morning, but she didn't meet any patients.
5. At the restaurant, Mustafa made the soup and the salad.
6. Anatoly drinks coffee or tea.

Exercise 3 page 95
1. Dora went to the meeting, but she didn't take notes.
2. Adam checked the office e-mail and went to the meeting.
3. Rachel prepared the meeting room, but she didn't make the coffee.
4. Dora and Adam went to the meeting, but they didn't prepare the meeting room.
5. Adam took notes and made copies.

6. Rachel picked up supplies and delivered the mail.

Exercise 4 page 95

1. and
2. or
3. and
4. but

Lesson D: Reading

Exercise 1 page 96

1. c
2. b
3. c
4. a
5. b
6. a

Exercise 2 page 96

1. Carrie McIntosh wrote the letter.
2. She wrote it on May 25, 2013.
3. She teaches at Westport Community College.
4. She teaches in the Medical Assistant Certificate Program.
5. manage a medical office, schedule appointments, and take care of patient records

Exercise 3 page 97

1. e
2. h
3. c
4. a
5. b
6. d
7. g
8. f

Exercise 4 page 97

1. homemaker
2. construction worker
3. orderly
4. medical assistant
5. auto mechanic
6. teacher
7. cashier
8. cook

Lesson E: Writing

Exercise 1 page 98

1. works
2. makes
3. answers
4. takes
5. prepares
6. assists
7. worked
8. was
9. handled
10. operated
11. was
12. went
13. was
14. graduated
15. got

Exercise 2 page 98

1. He started his job at the medical clinic in 2008.
2. He worked at Freshie's Pizza for 12 years.
3. He was a student from 2006 to 2008.
4. He studied for his GED at Staples Adult School.
5. He got his GED in June 2003.
6. He works at Valley Medical Clinic now.

Exercise 3 page 99

1. I prepared food, but I didn't clear the tables.
2. I handled money and talked to people every day.
3. I helped the nurses, but I didn't help the doctors.
4. I took care of my children and my house.
5. I cleared tables and handled money, but I didn't prepare food.
6. I operated large machines and built houses.

Exercise 4 page 99

a. 3: orderly
b. 1: cook
c. 5: busperson
d. 2: cashier
e. 6: construction worker
f. 4: homemaker

Lesson F: Another view

Exercise 1 page 100

1. Orderly
2. Cashier
3. Construction Worker
4. Medical Assistant
5. Auto Mechanic
6. Busperson

Exercise 2 page 100

1. orderly
2. construction worker
3. cashier
4. auto mechanic
5. busperson
6. construction worker
7. medical assistant
8. busperson

Exercise 3 page 101

1. couldn't, can
2. could, can't
3. couldn't, can't
4. could, can't
5. could, can
6. couldn't, can
7. couldn't, can
8. couldn't, can

Unit 9: Daily living

Lesson A: Listening

Exercise 1 page 102

1. lightbulb
2. sink
3. dishwasher
4. leak
5. lock
6. garbage
7. washing machine
8. dryer

Exercise 2 page 102

1. garbage
2. lock
3. lightbulb
4. sink
5. dishwasher
6. leak
7. washing machine
8. dryer

Exercise 3 page 103

1. She has five appliances in her kitchen.
2. She has a washing machine, a dryer, a stove, a refrigerator, and a dishwasher.
3. Two appliances have problems.
4. The dishwasher and the washing machine have problems.

Exercise 4 page 103

1. b
2. a
3. c
4. b
5. c
6. b
7. a
8. a
9. c

Lesson B: Can you call a plumber, please?

Exercise 1 page 104

1. Could you call a plumber, please?
2. Would you fix the window, please?
3. Will you fix the lock, please?
4. Would you fix the dryer, please?
5. Could you unclog the sink, please?
6. Can you fix the stove, please?

Exercise 2 page 104

1. b
2. a
3. b
4. a
5. b
6. b

Exercise 3 page 105

1. Could you fix the window, please?
2. Would you repair the refrigerator, please?
3. Can you fix the light, please?
4. Will you unclog the sink, please?
5. Could you repair the lock, please?
6. Would you fix the dishwasher, please?

Exercise 4 page 105

1. Could you fix the light, please?
2. Could you unclog the bathtub, please?
3. Could you change the lightbulb, please?

4. Could you repair the dishwasher, please?
5. Could you clean the carpet, please?
6. Could you call a plumber, please?

Lesson C: Which one do you recommend?
Exercise 1 page 106
1. do; They recommend Jerry's Plumbing.
2. does; He recommends Joe Thompson.
3. do; I recommend Wired Electric.
4. do; They recommend Rite Price.
5. does; She recommends Bank and Trust.
6. does; He recommends SaveMore.

Exercise 2 page 106
1. Marian recommends her cousin.
2. I suggest Drains R Us.
3. He likes Ed Peterson.
4. She recommends Dr. White.
5. We like Food City.
6. She recommends Rockland Adult School.
7. We suggest the City Clinic.

Exercise 3 page 107
1. ABC
2. ABC
3. Fix It
4. Fix It

Exercise 4 page 107
1. I recommend All Keys because it's open 24 hours.
2. They suggest Smitty's because it's licensed.
3. Harry likes All Keys because it's more experienced.
4. Muriel suggests Smitty's because it gives free keys.
5. They recommend All Keys because it has fast service.

Lesson D: Reading
Exercise 1 page 108
1. b 3. a 5. b
2. b 4. c 6. a

Exercise 2 page 109
1. burned out 6. jammed
2. broken 7. torn
3. dripping 8. scratched
4. bent 9. stained
5. cracked

Exercise 3 page 109
1. jammed 6. cracked
2. broken 7. bent
3. burned out 8. stained
4. dripping 9. scratched
5. torn

Lesson E: Writing
Exercise 1 page 110
1. broken 5. burned out
2. cracked 6. dripping
3. stained 7. scratched
4. jammed 8. clogged

Exercise 2 page 110
1. Three signatures
2. 201, 412, 605, 822
3. December 2, 2013
4. Ms. Torrant
5. Sincerely
6. Three paragraphs.
7. Jim Bowen

Exercise 3 page 111
1. cracked bathtub
2. dishwasher
3. leaking
4. clogged toilet
5. stove
6. broken
7. carpet
8. stained

Lesson F: Another view
Exercise 1 page 112
1. C 3. D 5. C
2. A 4. B 6. D

Exercise 2 page 113
1. Let's fix, let's fix
2. Let's buy, let's not buy, Let's clean
3. Let's buy, let's not buy, Let's make
4. Let's buy, Let's buy
5. Let's clean, Let's buy

Unit 10: Free time
Lesson A: Listening
Exercise 1 page 114
1. balloons
2. flowers
3. a card
4. perfume
5. a cake
6. a piece of cake
7. a guest
8. a present

Exercise 2 page 115

Exercise 3 page 115
1. T 4. T 7. F
2. F 5. F 8. T
3. F 6. F 9. T

Lesson B: Would you like some cake?
Exercise 1 page 116
1. Would you like some cake?
2. Would they like some coffee?
3. Would you like some ice cream?
4. Would she like a balloon?
5. Would they like some flowers?
6. Would you like some dessert?
7. Would he like a cup of tea?

Exercise 2 page 116
1. a 3. a 5. a 7. b
2. b 4. b 6. a 8. b

Exercise 3 page 117
1. They'd like some soda.
2. He'd like some coffee.
3. We'd like some salad.
4. she'd like a hot dog.
5. I'd like some fruit.
6. I'd like some cheese.

Exercise 4 page 117
1. What would you
2. I would like
3. Would you like
4. thank you
5. Would you like
6. I'd like
7. Would you like
8. I'd like
9. What would they

Lesson C: Tim gave Mary a present.
Exercise 1 page 118
1. Tim gave Mary a present.
2. Jim bought Sarah some flowers.
3. Elias wrote his father an e-mail.
4. Marta bought her son some soda.

5. Felix gave his children some ice cream.
6. Liu-na sent her mother a birthday card.

Exercise 2 page 118
1. Tim gave her a present.
2. Jim bought her some flowers.
3. Elias wrote him an e-mail.
4. Marta bought him some soda.
5. Felix gave them some ice cream.
6. Liu-na sent her a birthday card.

Exercise 3 page 119
1. barbecue grill
2. a salad bowl
3. linens
4. coffee cups
5. a check

Exercise 4 page 119
1. Mina's parents gave them a check.
2. Penny gave them coffee cups.
3. Maria gave them a salad bowl.
4. Mina's sister gave them towels.

Lesson D: Reading
Exercise 1 page 120
1. Halloween.
2. Last night.
3. The children.
4. Do-cheon.
5. Stayed home and gave out candy.
6. About a month.

Exercise 2 page 120
1. d	4. g	7. c
2. a	5. b	8. f
3. i	6. h	9. e

Exercise 3 page 121
1. A wedding.
2. Thanksgiving.
3. Halloween.

4. Mother's Day.
5. New Year's Eve.
6. A baby shower.

Exercise 4 page 121
Parties
a baby shower
a housewarming
New Year's Eve
a wedding
No school or work
Independence Day
Thanksgiving
Give presents or cards
a baby shower
a housewarming
Mother's Day
Valentine's Day
a wedding

Lesson E: Writing
Exercise 1 page 122
1. Thank you for the interesting book you gave me.
2. I'm really excited about reading it.
3. Thank you for bringing a cake to our party.
4. I really liked it a lot.
5. Thank you for coming to my graduation party.
6. I hope you had a good time.

Exercise 2 page 122
1. Thank you for the interesting book you gave me.
2. I'm really excited about reading it.
3. thank you for bringing a cake to our party.
4. I really liked it a lot.
5. Thank you for coming to my graduation party.
6. I hope you had a good time.

Exercise 3 page 123
1. It was Joe's party.
2. He wrote it on June 15, 2013.
3. He wrote it to Erica.
4. Erica gave him a book.
5. Erica brought a chocolate cake to the party.
6. Joe liked the cake because chocolate is his favorite kind of cake.

Exercise 4 page 123
1. Dan
2. chocolates
3. Valentine's Day
4. favorite
5. Thank you
6. hope

Lesson F: Another view
Exercise 1 page 124
1. A	3. A	5. C	7. A
2. C	4. B	6. D	8. A

Exercise 2 page 125
1. There were
2. There was
3. There were
4. There was
5. There wasn't any
6. There weren't any
7. There are
8. There is
9. There aren't any
10. There isn't any
11. There is
12. There are